In Detail 2

English for Global Communication

Isobel Rainey de Diaz

with
Kristin L. Johannsen

THOMSON
HEINLE

United States · Australia · Canada · Mexico · Singapore · Spain · United Kingdom

THOMSON

HEINLE

In Detail 2
Isobel Rainey de Diaz

Publisher: *Chris Wenger*
Editorial Manager: *Berta de Llano*
Senior Development Editor: *Jean Pender*
Director ELT/ESL Marketing: *Amy Mabley*
Development Editor: *Ivor Williams*
Sr. Production Editor: *Sally Cogliano*
Manufacturing Coordinator: *Mary Beth Hennebury*
Cover Image: *"Digital Highway" by Todd Davidson*
Compositor: *Graphic World*
Project Manager: *Kris Swanson*
Photography Manager: *Sheri Blaney*

Illustrator: *Raketshop*
Cover Designer: *Joseph Sherman*
Interior Designer: *Jean Hammond*
Printer: *R.R. Donnelley*
Also participating in the publication of this program were:
Directors of ELT: *Jim Goldstone, John Lowe*
ELT Academic and Training Director: *Francisco Lozano*
ELT Marketing Managers: *Eric Bredenberg, Ian Martin, Irina Pereyra*
Editorial: *Sean Bermingham, Paul MacIntyre, Stephanie Schmidt, Carmen Corral-Reid, Lisa Geraghty*

Printed in China by R.R. Donnelley
2 3 4 5 6 7 8 9 10 and 06 05 04

For more information contact Thomson Heinle, 25 Thomson Place, Boston, Massachusetts 02210 USA, or you can visit our Internet site at http://www.heinle.com

0-8384-4557-8

Photo Credits: All photographs not credited are the exclusive property of Heinle. ISI=Index Stock Imagery
1: Reuters NewMedia Inc./CORBIS, tl: Wally McNamee/CORBIS, bl, br: Reuters NewMedia Inc./CORBIS; **2:** Ohlinger Jerry/CORBIS SYGMA; **4:** Ohlinger Jerry/CORBIS SYGMA; **6:** Gary Conner/ISI (Index Stock Imagery); **7:** t: AFP/CORBIS, b: CORBIS SYGMA; **8:** both: Reuters NewMedia Inc./CORBIS; **9:** Photoplay Archives/CORBIS; **10:** t to b: Reuters NewMedia Inc./CORBIS, Wally McNamee/CORBIS, Reuters NewMedia Inc./Corbis, Bradley Smith/CORBIS, John Atashian/CORBIS, Mitch Jacobson/Associated Press; **12:** bl: Dave Bantruff/ISI, tl: Stuart Westmoreland/ISI, tr: RO-MA Stock/ISI; **14:** Kindra Clineff/ISI; **17:** Jacob Halaska/ISI; **18:** l: Steve Dunwell Photography Inc./ISI; r: Eva Amiya/ISI; **19:** RO-MA Stock/ISI; **21:** tl: Yvette Cardozo/ISI, tr: GETTY RF, r: Profolio Enr./ISI, b: Corinne Humphrey/ISI; **24:** t: Rob & Ann Simpson/Visuals Unlimited; **26:** Wilson Goodrich/ISI; **28:** l: Leonard de Selva/CORBIS, r: Bettmann/CORBIS; **29:** Frank Perkins/ISI; **33:** l: Mitchell Gerber/CORBIS, r: Trapper Frank/CORBIS SYGMA; **34:** Richard Orton/ISI; **35:** l: Walter Bibikow/ISI; **38:** Charles Benes/ISI; **40:** l: ASAP Ltd./ISI; c: Phil Kember/ISI; r: Rose/ISI; b: E.J. West/ISI; **41:** Jeff Greenberg/ISI; **42:** Gary Isaacs/ ISI; **44:** bl: Tom Carroll/ISI; br: Keren Su/ISI; **45:** l: Bettmann/CORBIS; c: Peter Turnley/CORBIS; r: Peter Turnley/CORBIS; **49:** Bettmann/CORBIS; **50:** tl and tr: ASAP Ltd./ISI; b: Peter Turnley/CORBIS; **51:** t: Getty RF; b: Bonnie Kamin/ISI; **52:** l: Jack Hollingsworth/CORBIS; c: Gary D. Landsman/CORBIS; **54:** tl: Omni Photo Communications Inc./ISI; tr:Vic Bider/ISI; b: Lynn Goldsmith/CORBIS; **58:** Bruce Clarke/ISI; **60:** Getty RF; **61:** r: Inga Spence/ISI; **62:** David Jentz/ISI; **63:** Jeff Greenberg/ISI; **64:** bl: Henryk Kaiser/ISI; br: Walter Bibikow/ISI; **67:** l: Getty RF; **68:** Bettmann/CORBIS; **70:** t: Stanley Rowin/ISI; b: Richard Wood/ISI; **74:** Getty RF; **75:** Lou Jones/ISI; **77:** Katie Deits/ISI; **78:** t: Frank Simonetti; b: Jacob Halaska/ISI; **79:** tl: Food Pix; tr: David Burch/ISI; bl: Food Pix; br: Howard Sokol/ISI; **80:** Zefa Visual Media; **81:** Eddie Stangler/ISI; Patrick Giardino/CORBIS; **84:** Robert Caputo/Aurora; **85:** Index RF; **86:** t: Gary Conner/ISI; b: Hoa Qui/ISI; **88:** Gary Conner/ISI; **89:** tr: Keith Wood/Visuals Unlimited; bl: Jackson Lab/Visuals Unlimited; **90:** Benelux Press/ISI; **91:** Najlah/CORBIS SABA; **94:** l to r: Getty RF, Robert Franz/ISI, Volvox/ISI; **95:** Jacob Halaska/ISI; **96:** l: Lou Jones/ISI; **97:** Tom Carter/ISI; **98:** Steve/Mary Skjold/ISI; **101:** 2nd from l: Comstock RF; **103:** clockwise from tl: Paul A. Souders/CORBIS, Michael S. Yamashita/CORBIS, Peter Turnley/CORBIS, Owen Franken/CORBIS; Zefa Visual Media-Germany/ISI; **104:** Lawrence Sawyer/ISI; **107:** Stewart Cohen/ISI; **108:** l: Raeanne Rubenstein/ISI, r: Barbara Haynor/ISI; **109:** t: Inc., HMS Group/ISI; **110:** l to r: Stocktrek/CORBIS, AFP/CORBIS, Getty RF, Lauree Feldman/ISI; **113:** l: Chip Henderson/ISI; r: Jim Lo Scalzo/Aurora; **116:** Daniel Morrison/ISI; **118:** tl: Bill Bachmann/ISI; cl: Nancy Sheehan/ISI; cr top: Joanna B. Pinneo/Aurora; cr bottom: Caleb Kenna/Aurora; **119:** Sheri Blaney/ISI; **120:** Chip Henderson/ISI; **122:** Chip Henderson/ISI; **123:** l: AFP/CORBIS; c: CORBIS; **128:** l: Getty RF; c: Kevin Fleming/CORBIS; r: Lou Jones/ISI; **132:** Rich Remsberg/ISI

Text Credits: **12:** "Where the heart is," by Maureen Rice, from *The Guardian*, 23 December, 2002 © Maureen Rice; **22:** "Feel the heat" by Richard Wentk, from *Focus Magazine*, March 2002; **36:** "Greenhouse melts Alaska's tribal ways," by Duncan Campbell, from *The Guardian,,* 16 July 2002, © Guardian; **46:***Assembling the Future: How International Migrants Are Shaping the 21st Century,"* by Roger Doyle, © 2002 Roger Doyle; **80:** "Chocolate town goes up for sale," by Neil Buckley and Ien Cheng, from *Financial Times*, July 28, 2002; **104:** "Accidents of birth, brother where art thou?," by Paul Sieveking, from *Fortean Times Magazine, World of Strange Phenomenon*, August 2002; **105:** "Wild things/ wild things worldwide," by Paul Sieveking, from *Fortean Times Magazine, World of Strange Phenomenon*, August 2002; **114:** "Shepherd school," by James Astill, from *The Guardian*, 12 April 2002 © James Astill; **124:** "100 young inventors," from *Technology Review*, June, 2002 © *technology Review;*

Author's Acknowledgments

While writing this series, the author was Visiting ESP Lecturer in the Escuela Universitaria de Ingeniería Técnica Minera at the University of León, Spain. She would like to express her gratitude to the Director of the School Don Fernando Fernández San Elías for his encouragement, and for the confidence he showed her in allowing her access to her office at the weekends. She is also indebted to the Director of Studies Don Gustavo Elízaga Antón for his practical support, and to all her colleagues, administrative staff, teachers and students, in the School for their cheerful cooperation inside and outside the classroom.

The author also wishes to acknowledge that, while writing the series, her family—Pedro Agustín, Julian, Ivan, Jan and Jo—have been a major source of inspiration and fortitude.

Sincere thanks are also due to the editorial team Berta, Jean, and Ruth and support author Kristin for their singleminded determination not just to produce a wonderful upper intermediate/advanced series but to get it published on schedule!

In addition to the above, we would like to extend our thanks to the following professionals who have offered invaluable comments and suggestions during the development of this series:

Nicolas Baychelier, *Chung Yuan Christian University, Taiwan*

Andrew Berriman, *Shih Hsin University, Taiwan*

Grazyna Anna Bonomi, *Yázigi Internexus, Brasil*

An-Jean Chiang, *Yuan Ze University, Taiwan*

Tania Cvihun Kedzior, *ITESM Prepa Tec Eugenio Garza Sada, México*

Tamaki Harrold, *Simul Academy, Japan*

Margaret B. Hug, *ESL Specialist Program, U.S. Consulate, México*

Patricia Lálange del Vall, *Instituto de Enseñanza Superior del Ejército, Argentina*

Patricia Alejandra Lastiri, *Instituto de Enseñanza Superior del Ejército, Argentina*

Han-yi Lin, Language Center, *National Cheng-chi University, Taiwan*

Ramiro Luna Rivera, *ITESM, México*

Maria Teresa Maiztegui, *Uniao Cultural Brasil Estados Unidos, Brasil*

Claudia Marín Cabrera, *Comunidad Educativa Diocesana El Buen Pastor / Pontificia Universidad Católica del Peru*

Maria Ordoñez, *Universidad de Celaya, México*

Stephen Shrader, *Language Institute of Japan*

Kang-Jen Tien, *Chang-Gung University, Taiwan*

Maria Christina Uchoa Close, *Instituto Cultural Brasil-Estados Unidos, Brasil*

Table of Contents

People

1 Warm Up

A. PAIR WORK Describe the people in these pictures. Do you recognize them? What do they do for a living? Do you think they are happy or unhappy people? Give reasons for your speculations.

B. Talk about the professions in the box below, using adjectives from the box in exercise C. Some adjectives can be used with several professions.

> movie star   international soccer player   politician
> doctor   astronaut   research scientist
> dot-com entrepreneur   homemaker   TV host
> war correspondent

C. Most of the adjectives used in B describe permanent qualities. Other adjectives in the box below describe feelings and temporary emotional states. Put them under the appropriate headings.

> patient determined caring energetic healthy wise courageous
> adventurous creative entertaining outgoing well-organized
> thorough good-looking disciplined careful ambitious inquisitive
> unselfish talented pleased annoyed worried relaxed depressed
> excited indignant sad nervous furious unconfident confused
> disgusted delighted heartbroken relieved miserable

Feeling down	Feeling insecure	Feeling angry	Feeling good

D. Now look again at the pictures of the famous people and use these adjectives to talk about their lives.

EXAMPLE: *Christopher Reeve must have been delighted when he got to play the role of Superman.*

FYI   inquisitive = likes asking questions and finding things out

Reading strategy

Looking for patterns in reading texts

A writer often puts together a piece of writing using a particular structure or pattern. Sometimes a writer presents a series of problems and their solutions. Other common patterns a writer uses are "for and against," "the past compared to now," and "advantages versus disadvantages." Understanding these rhetorical patterns can help you to understand a text more fully.

Before you read

A. PAIR WORK Use the following information to write at least six logical sentences about the life of Christopher Reeve.

1952	Manhattan
English and music	Cornell University
drama	Juilliard School
four Superman movies	1995
accident	now
Christopher Reeve Paralysis Foundation	

First reading

B. Scan the text and check whether the sentences you wrote in exercise A are factually correct.

THE ADVENTURE CONTINUES

SUPERMAN II

Superman, Superhero

Until the mid-90s, Christopher Reeve was known mostly for his performance as Superman on the silver screen, but a tragic accident changed all that. A keen equestrian, Reeve was thrown from his horse in
5 1995 and left paralyzed from the neck down.

Born in 1952 in Manhattan, Reeve's first great challenge in life was to try and come to terms with the break-up of his parents' marriage when he was still only a small child and which caused him lasting distress. As a
10 young adult he found consolation in sailing, swimming, and the theater and eventually studied English and music theory at Cornell University before being selected to study drama at New York's elite° Juilliard School.

Despite a Broadway appearance alongside Katherine
15 Hepburn, his early years as an actor were difficult. During his first attempt to make it in Hollywood, for example, he suffered a total loss of motivation, which almost ended his acting career. In 1977, however, he decided to try again. He got a part in an off-Broadway
20 production and while he was working on the show, he screen-tested for the role of Superman. Thanks to his thorough preparation and resemblance to the original comic-strip hero, Reeve was given the part.

The outstanding box-office success of the film
25 *Superman* was largely due to Reeve's witty° portrayal of the Man of Steel, and four films later, he was one of Tinseltown's richest stars. The years between *Superman* and his accident were, however, less
30 rewarding in both acting and economic terms. Unable to "escape the cape" as Reeve himself
35 put it, he was offered only limited roles. Ironically, one such role in a TV movie was that of a crooked ex-cop, who pretended to be paralyzed.
40 The movie *Above Suspicion* was shown the week before Reeve's accident.

Reeve's injuries were so severe that he stopped breathing for three minutes and his head had to be reattached to his spinal column. Worst of all, his spinal
45 cord° was severed. The spinal cord is an extremely delicate part of the body. It is only fractions of a centimeter in diameter and if damaged, it does not regenerate itself. Thus, nerve signals, which allow us to feel and move, can no longer be sent to the brain. With
50 the help of his loving and supportive wife Dana, Reeve came through near-suicidal° depression and learned to accept that he was paralyzed and dependent on others to keep him alive and breathing with the aid of an oxygen tube.

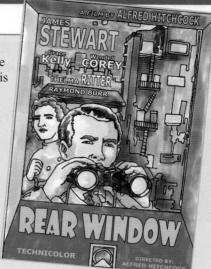

55 With characteristic determination, Reeve returned to his acting career, appearing in a remake of the Hitchcock film *Rear Window*. But he had discovered a new interest: medical research. In 1996, he founded his own Christopher Reeve Foundation, which subsequently
60 merged, in 1999, with the American Paralysis Foundation to become the Christopher Reeve Paralysis Foundation. Through the foundation, Reeve has raised enormous amounts of money for research into the development of effective treatments for spinal cord injury paralysis and
65 supports, for example, the controversial work, carried out in some countries, into stem cells° derived from cloned° human embryos. The foundation also supports more recent research, done mostly in Australia, into injecting cells from a paralyzed patient's nose into the spinal cord.
70 Unlike other cells in the human body, nose cells continue to regenerate throughout life, so it is hoped that the transplanted cells will allow the spinal nerves to grow again.

Whether Reeve walks again or not, one thing is
75 certain. He may no longer be Superman on screen, but his courage in the face of adversity and his determination to improve his
80 quality of life and that of other paralyzed people make him a superhero in
85 real life.

elite = select, privileged part of a larger body or group
witty = humorous in a clever way
spinal cord = cord of nerves that runs through the spine, connecting different parts of the body with the brain
suicidal = having a tendency to commit suicide (take one's own life)
stem cell = undifferentiated cell from which specialized cells develop
to clone = to make a duplicate copy of a living thing

Second reading

C. Complete the outline.

Christopher Reeve

Personal data:
  a. Date of birth _____
  b. Place of birth _____
  c. Marital status _____

Education:
  d. _____
  e. _____

Acting experience:
  f. *Acted on and off Broadway.*
  g. _____ movies, e.g., 1. _____ 2. _____

Other interests:
  h. _____

Problems and solutions:
  i. _____
  j. _____
  k. _____

Vocabulary in context

D. Find words or phrases in the text that mean the same or nearly the same as these.

1. to renew
2. representation
3. a horse rider
4. very bad luck
5. exceptional
6. unable to move
7. to accept
8. dishonest
9. cut through/off
10. informal name for Hollywood
11. extreme unhappiness
12. combined/joined

Discussion

E. Choose adjectives that you think describe Reeve's personal qualities. Find sections in the text that justify your choices.

Review of tenses: Past perfect progressive

Practice

A. Use these descriptions to identify the tense and voice of the statements.

simple present tense active voice

simple past tense active voice

present perfect active voice

future tense active voice

simple present tense passive voice

simple past tense passive voice

past progressive active voice

past perfect active voice

EXAMPLES:

1. *Reeve was thrown from his horse in 1995.*   *simple past tense passive voice*
2. *The foundation supports medical research.*   *simple present tense active voice*

1. His parents' marital problems caused him lasting distress.
2. Reeve has raised enormous amounts of money for medical research.
3. He was working on an off-Broadway production.
4. He had discovered a new interest: medical research.
5. He was given the part of Superman in 1977.
6. His injuries were severe.
7. The spinal cord is an extremely delicate part of the human body.
8. Nose cells are injected into the spinal cord.
9. At the time of his accident, Reeve was participating in horse trials.
10. Despite the obstacles, Reeve will continue to support research.

B. Read the statements and match these symbols with each part of the statement.

continuous past action

X = completed action in the past

EXAMPLE:

Reeve had been living life to the fullest before he suffered the riding accident.
a. *Reeve had been living life to the fullest* ∿→
b. *. . . he suffered the riding accident.* X

1. Reeve had been studying English at Cornell before he was selected for Juilliard.
2. When I met my friend, she had been shopping.
3. We decided to leave New York after we had been living there for several years.

4. Because it had been raining, the streets were wet.
5. I had just been thinking about you when you called.
6. They had been operating for almost an hour when the patient had a heart attack.
7. Before he got his big break, Reeve had been acting for some time.
8. When they interviewed his wife after the accident, she had been crying.

C. Read the statements in exercise B again and classify each one under the correct heading below.

Action that went on for a long time in the past before another action occurred

_____

_____

Action that went on for a long time in the past and was interrupted by another past action

_____

_____

Action that went on for a long time in the past and stopped, but when the other action occurred, there was still evidence of the continuous action

_____

_____

D. Which of the pairs of sentences are in (a) the present time frame, (b) the past time frame, or (c) the future time frame?

1. In 2002, we went to Seoul for the World Cup. We had never been there before.
2. I'll see him next week. He's going to be pleased.
3. The Christopher Reeve Paralysis Foundation has become important. It provides a lot of money for medical research.

E. Indicate whether these statements are correct (C) or incorrect (I). Correct the incorrect ones. Remember to consider the appropriate time frame for the verbs.

1. He is running his own business now; it's the first time he had worked in business.
2. Reeve was very depressed after his accident; he had never before been seriously ill.
3. After we have been riding for a long time, I was thrown off my horse.
4. I had been riding since I am a teenager.
5. I have just read the newspaper. The news will be interesting.
6. They were running along the street when the police stop them.
7. It's going to be very hot tomorrow; I go to the beach.
8. I'm going to Tokyo next week; I'll call you from my hotel.

Past perfect progressive

Form	Examples	Uses
past perfect of *be* (*had been*) + *-ing* form of the lexical verb	*When I saw Tom, he had clearly been dieting.*	1. continuous, completed past action with evidence of action still visible when another past action occurs
	I had been sleeping for a couple of hours when the phone rang.	2. continuous, incomplete past action interrupted by another past action
	Before he interviewed for the role of Superman, he had been working off-Broadway.	3. continuous past action completed just before another past action occurs

Test yourself

F. Complete the text with the correct tense of the verbs in parentheses. More than one answer may be possible in some cases.

Since his accident, Reeve **(1)** _____ (consider) medical research to be of vital importance to humanity. Over the past seven years, he **(2)** _____ (dedicate) most of his time and energy to his foundation, which **(3)** _____ (support) research into treatments for spinal cord injury paralysis. Before his accident, Reeve **(4)** _____ (work) mostly in the theater and movies, with his role as Superman making him very rich. He **(5)** _____ (enjoy) some success in TV when the terrible accident **(6)** _____ (occur). Although he was terribly depressed after the accident, he soon **(7)** _____ (recover) his optimistic spirit. He is now convinced that one day he **(8)** _____ (walk) again. Recently, he has been able to move his fingers for the first time since the accident.

Speaking focus

Managing conversations

These expressions are helpful when you need clarification. When you want the speaker to repeat something: *Pardon? Excuse me? Would you repeat that?* (Use rising, question intonation.)

When someone is speaking very fast: *Could you please speak a little more slowly? Would you mind speaking a bit more slowly?*

When you don't understand a word: *What does ... mean? Could you explain what you mean by ...?*

Think about it

A. PAIR WORK Make notes about obstacles that people sometimes face in reaching their goals, such as overcoming illnesses. Then share your ideas with a partner. Which obstacles are the most serious? Use expressions from the box to manage the conversation, when appropriate.

B. PAIR WORK Situation: You are officers of an organization called Bright Futures. Every year, Bright Futures gives one student a scholarship to attend a university. Read the biographies of the candidates and choose two to recommend for a scholarship. Make notes of your reasons.

Student 1:
Sonia got married right after she graduated from high school and has two children, ages three and one. Her husband died last year in a car accident. She lives with her parents now. She wants to major in education so she can work as a teacher to support her children.

Student 2:
Dan is the oldest of eight brothers and sisters. He loves art and draws and paints beautifully. He has already won several art contests. His father is a factory worker and can't afford to pay for his children's education. Dan hopes to attend art college and become a professional artist.

Student 3:
Maya came to this country as a refugee. No one in her family has ever attended a university. She failed some high school classes. She says this was because she had to work at night to earn money for her family. She wants to study business administration and start her own company, to give jobs to women.

Student 4:
Victor can't walk and has been using a wheelchair since he was a little boy. He has received excellent grades in his science classes. He hopes to attend medical school and become a doctor, so that he can help other people with disabilities.

C. GROUP WORK Now work together with another pair. Choose the person who will get the scholarship and prepare a short report explaining your decision and reasons. Then take turns giving your reports to the class. Did any groups make the same decision? Did you have the same reasons?

In the U.S., 6% of college students receive scholarships from private organizations to help them pay for their educations. In 2002, the average amount of a scholarship was $2,051.

FYI Parkinson's disease is an illness in the body's nervous system

A. Read the paragraphs and try to understand the meanings of the words and expressions in **bold.**

Many people believe that Michael J. Fox is **fighting a losing battle** in his attempts to find a cure for his and other people's Parkinson's disease, but Fox **soldiers on,** refusing to **give up hope.** Of course, there are times when he **despairs of** ever living a completely normal life again, but his determination and optimism help him **come through** these difficult periods, although he himself says that it is his wife's support that has been **the key to** his positive attitude.

Facing up to the fact that you have **a critical illness** such as cancer, or that you have **a permanent disability** as a result of a serious injury or accident can be a very **traumatic** experience. Fortunately, many health services have **support systems** that help people deal with their worst fears and confused emotions at such times. In some health centers in many countries, laughter clinics have been set up within the main hospital complex because research has shown that if seriously ill patients laugh a lot, they are likely to **recover from** their illness. Researchers believe that, as the patients laugh, the depression from which many of them are suffering lifts. This can **boost** their immune systems, which then start to fight the disease.

B. Complete the statements with the correct form of a word or expression from exercise A.

1. If doctors think you might die of your condition, then you have _____.

2. Research has shown that people who never _____ are more likely to live longer than those who become depressed because of their illness.

3. Doctors in the 1970s were amazed to discover that patients who laughed a lot often _____ their illnesses even when the illnesses were critical.

4. If you have _____, you will have to live with your medical condition for the rest of your life.

5. When sick people get good news about their health, this can _____ their self-confidence and help them get better more quickly.

6. If you are very unlikely to succeed at something but keep on trying, people less optimistic than you will say you are _____.

7. When a person continues to try to do something even though it is difficult or painful, then he or she _____.

8. A good researcher never _____ finding solutions to the problems he or she is studying.

9. Most people who have _____ periods of difficulties in their lives say that _____ their survival was the support of family and friends.

10. Hospitals and other _____ help patients and their families understand better the _____ experiences of serious illness.

C. PAIR WORK Think about a difficult time in your life or in the life of a close relative that you or your relative came through successfully. Work with a friend in your class and tell each other about this experience. Try to include words and expressions from exercise A.

D. Circle the correct interpretation of *the idioms* in these statements.

1. I really *blew it* at that job interview.
My performance was *good.*
My performance was *poor.*

2. She's going to try to *make it* in New York.
She's going to try to *be a success.*
She's going to try to *make friends.*

3. I think I'm *losing it.*
I *am in complete control* of my life.
I *no longer have control* of my life.

Listening
strategy

Listening and taking notes on a talk

When you take notes on a lecture or conversation, you write down the most important information. Remember, good notes don't need complete sentences—just words and phrases.

Before you listen

A. PAIR WORK Do you know of any famous people in your country who faced some serious problems? How did they overcome their problems?

First listening

B. You are going to hear a biography of the American TV celebrity Oprah Winfrey. Listen and answer True (T) or False (F). If the sentence is false, change it to make it true.

1. Oprah grew up in one of the richest areas of the United States.
2. Oprah's mother helped her to change her life when she was fourteen.
3. Oprah started working at a TV station after she graduated from college.
4. People can watch Oprah's TV program in 106 cities around the world.
5. Oprah has given millions of dollars to help old people in many countries.

Second listening

C. Listen again and take notes for each of these things. Write only words and phrases—not complete sentences.

People who helped Oprah _____

Kinds of work Oprah has done _____

How Oprah helps people now _____

After listening

D. Are there any famous people in your country who have given money to help others? What have they done?

Test yourself

E. Listen to this biography of Stephen Hawking and take short notes.

His occupation _____

His problem _____

Things he can't do _____

His activities (4) _____

_____

How many words are in your notes?

_____

Writing short life histories

Before you write

A. GROUP WORK Classify the statements below as narrative, descriptive, or expository. Put the number of the statement under the correct heading. As you do this activity, discuss the reasons for your choices.

| FYI | Expository discourse is concerned with telling what something is, defining and explaining. |

Narrative	Descriptive	Expository

1. Reeve used to be tall, slim, and very athletic.
2. After she was diagnosed with drug and alcohol problems, Betty Ford, former First Lady of the White House, went into a rehab center.
3. Alzheimer's disease is common among people between the ages of 65 and 80.
4. When those cancer patients went to the laughter clinic, their attitude toward life began to change, and as the laughter treatment had its effect, their illnesses became less serious.
5. The atmosphere in laughter clinics is relaxed and welcoming, and the health workers who work there are cheerful and caring.
6. Because it carries important messages to the brain, the spinal cord is vital to our survival.

B. Read the text and decide which parts are mostly narrative, which mostly descriptive, and which mostly expository.

Elvis Presley

Although he has been dead for over twenty-five years, Elvis Presley is still considered the king of rock-and-roll. What's more, his music is still popular with people of all ages, backgrounds, and nationalities. Elvis 5 was a charismatic singer who had a special connection with his audiences. He was also a patriotic U.S. citizen, who insisted on doing his military service like any other U.S. citizen. He was sent to Germany where he entertained his fellow GIs with 10 his songs. While he was there, he learned German and even had a couple of hit songs in that language.

Write

C. Think of a person who has influenced you a lot, for example, a singer, a politician, a teacher, a scientist, a sports personality, or a writer. Write about the person. Use the following outline.

Greatest Influence on My Life

a. *Expository mini text:* Identify the person; make a general statement about who he or she is or was; make a more specific statement about how he or she influences people.

b. *Descriptive mini text:* Describe the person's qualities and physical characteristics.

c. *Narrative mini text:* Talk about an important event in the person's life.

A. PAIR WORK Choose a famous person who has overcome adversity. The adversity does not have to be an illness or an accident. It could be business failure, loss of employment, or a personal scandal.

Make outline notes about the person. Use the outline notes to practice narrating to one another the person's story. Do not write the whole story. Then join up with another pair of students and listen to one another's stories.

B. GROUP WORK Brainstorm and list the diseases or illnesses that most affect your country. Complete the outline notes, but feel free to add your own sections.

Most common diseases in our country:
  a. say what they are
  b. say how many people they affect
  c. say what kind of people they affect

Effects of disease:
  d. describe the physical effects of the diseases
  e. describe the emotional side effects

Illustrations:
  f. tell the story of a person (or people) you know who has (have) suffered from the disease
  g. tell about the efforts of researchers to find cures and successful treatments

C. CLASS TASK Discuss this topic: Most money spent on medical research is wasted. In order to avoid many serious illnesses, governments should spend more money on educating people to take better care of themselves.

For more details about People, view the CNN video. Activities to accompany the video begin on page 137.

1. Oprah Winfrey
2. Christopher Reeve
3. Stephen Hawking
4. Helen Keller
5. Andrea Bocelli
6. Marlee Maitlin

Home

1 Warm Up

A. GROUP WORK Describe the pictures and say whether or not you would like to live permanently in each place. Give reasons for your preferences. Who do you think chooses to live in these places?

B. PAIR WORK Match the definitions below with the words in the box.

1. house that is divided and has two homes in it
2. house that is independent of other houses
3. home in a large building
4. small pretty house in the country
5. one-room house sometimes made of mud
6. house built on one level
7. house that shares two walls with other houses in a line of houses
8. house that is also a vehicle
9. portable shelter
10. place to keep cars, vans, and other vehicles

garage   tent   ranch house   duplex   apartment   mobile home   cottage
detached house   row house   hut

C. GROUP WORK Choose the most popular place to live from exercise B. List all the reasons why it is popular. Join a group with a different preference and try to convince them that your choice is better.

Before you read

A. GROUP WORK Match the words in the box with their definitions.

dwelling	home	accommodation	shelter	household

1. general word for a place to stay, usually not on a permanent basis
2. any construction where people can live
3. any building or covering that gives protection, for example, from the rain
4. people living together in one home
5. place where people feel they belong psychologically and emotionally

First reading

B. The reading deals with the concept and origins of the word *home*. Decide whether you think the following information is Correct *(C)* or Incorrect *(I)*. Then scan the text to find out whether your predictions were correct. Discuss with the other students any information in the text that you find surprising.

1. The house where you lived as a child will always be your home. _____
2. Home is where your parents are / one of your parents is. _____
3. It is a good idea to consider the workplace a substitute for home. _____
4. Home can be many things: a neighborhood, a relationship, a memory. _____
5. Homeless children often suffer major insecurities as adults. _____
6. The concept of home is very old and goes back to the Middle Ages. _____

Where the heart is . . .

Home, in the truest sense of the word, is where we want to be. But where is "home"? That question used to be easier to answer than it is now. Home was where you grew up. Later it was the home you made
5 with your own family. But where is home if your parents broke up and you spent half the week with your Mum and the rest of it with your Dad? Or where is home if you move every few years because of your job? **It goes without saying** that a house is not a home, but can you
10 ever feel at home in a rented accommodation with somebody else's furniture? We live increasingly peripatetic° lifestyles, but this, according to psychologist Dr. Hall Beloff, "makes the idea of home more important, not less," and this is especially
15 the case in our 24/7° culture, as the boundaries between work and home grow **fuzzier.**

"We increasingly define ourselves by our work," says psychotherapist Oliver James, "which is a horrible con.° Achievement is not the same as fulfillment,°
20 colleagues are not the new friends, and work is not the new home, whatever anybody says. Work and working relationships, no matter how **cordial,** are basically about **status,** power, and competition. At work, we put on a series of different identities, depending on the

circumstances. But home is where you can express your real identity. We need the boundary between our private selves and our public selves."

Home might always be the place where you grew up or the place where you live now. It may not even be a place, but a person, or a relationship, or a memory. Mine isn't a house, but my family and the area of west London where I was brought up. For Hall Beloff, "It was always where my mother was, even long after I was married and had my own children." For a friend of mine, who lived on a series of army **bases** as a child and who has moved to a new house every two or three years for the past decade, home is where her children are. "Home," according to Dr. Barrie Gunter, a psychologist at the University of Sheffield, "is where you are most at ease, and where you feel safe and most yourself. It's always more than just a place. It's a personal territory."

To appreciate the real value of home, we should consider the consequences of being without it. "About a third of prison populations never had proper homes when they were children. At a very young age, they learned that they had no security, that they could not rely on anything. They are literally° and **psychically** homeless, which means that they are broken . . ." says James. Fortunately, we don't get just one shot at home. If we do not get the ideal early start, we can always **put down roots** later in life. For most of us, it won't even be a

choice so much as **a compulsion.** Even rough sleepers try to establish some sense of territory by returning again and again to the same spot and by collecting objects and making shelters, not just for practical reasons but to create some **version** of "home."

Home is so important and such an apparently basic human need that it is hard to believe that the concept as we know it now is only a few hundred years old. Into the Middle Ages, most people still lived in conditions so poor, without heating, light, or furniture, that concepts such as "home" or "family" did not exist. Up until the 17th century, even affluent households were public, feudal° affairs of one or two rooms, in which family, servants, and employees lived, ate, worked, and slept communally. Only in the past 300 years has the idea of a private personal life developed and the modern notion of home—as comfort, **retreat,** and private space—evolved.

(Abridged and adapted from "Where the heart is . . ." *The Observer Magazine,* December 23, 2001, page 12.)

---

peripatetic = constantly moving from place to place
24/7 = twenty-four hours a day, seven days a week
con = confidence trick, something that cheats or deceives people
fulfillment = feeling of satisfaction
literally = in fact, in reality
feudal system = social system in medieval Europe

Second reading

C. Read for specific details.

1. In paragraph 1, find two facts that explain why "the place we grew up" is no longer a satisfactory definition of "home."

2. In paragraph 2, find four differences between the workplace and home.

3. In paragraph 3, find a more modern concept of home than that mentioned in paragraphs 1 and 6.

4. In paragraph 4, find the reason why home is a basic human need and two pieces of evidence to support this claim.

5. In paragraph 5, find two facts that explain why the concept of home as we know it today did not exist until the 17th century.

Vocabulary in context

D. Match the words and expressions from the text in column 1 with the explanations or synonyms in column 2.

Column 1	Column 2
1. line 8: it goes without saying	a. variation
2. line 16: fuzzier	b. calm, safe place
3. line 22: cordial	c. less clear
4. line 23: status	d. irresistible impulse
5. line 35: bases	e. level of importance
6. line 47: psychically	f. evidently, clearly
7. line 50: put down roots	g. friendly
8. line 52: compulsion	h. establish a home or base
9. line 56: version	i. mentally
10. line 68: retreat	j. camps

Discussion

E. PAIR WORK Discuss which of the concepts of home in the text apply to your home. Tell each other why your home is what it is and where it is.

Clauses with *wish*

Initial *only* for emphasis

Practice

A. PAIR WORK Read the following statements and answer these questions about each one.

In which tense is the verb in *italics?*
Does the verb in *italics* refer to the future or to the past?
Is it possible or impossible to satisfy the wish in each case?

1. I wish I *didn't have to* live in a rented accommodation.
2. I wish I *were* rich enough to buy my own duplex.
3. Paul wishes his parents *hadn't broken up* when he was small.
4. We wish our neighbors *wouldn't talk* so loudly.
5. We wish we *had bought* a house in the country.
6. Those young people wish they *didn't have* to live in the streets.
7. Many governments wish they *could solve* the problem of homelessness.
8. I wish I *hadn't bought* such a big house. It's so expensive to run.
9. I wish I *knew* how to paint and decorate. I could save so much money if I did all my painting and decorating myself.
10. Sue wishes she *lived* closer to the center so that she could walk to work.

B. Complete each statement with the correct form and tense of the verb in parentheses.

1. I wish I _____(buy) this car. It uses too much gas.
2. Kate is in Japan at the moment and she wishes she _____(speak) Japanese.
3. They wish they _____(afford) to rent a small apartment.
4. We wish we _____ (work) in the country. Life in this big city is so stressful.
5. We wish we_____ (rent) such a big apartment. The rent is very high.
6. Many prisoners wish they _____ (have) a good home to go to after they serve their time in prison.
7. Paul wishes he _____ (study) engineering. He would have preferred to be a social worker.
8. I wish I _____ (eat) so much for dinner. I am feeling terrible!

Interact

C. PAIR WORK Write notes with true information about yourself using the headings below. Then work with a partner and tell each other about your desires and regrets.

My desires	My regrets	My partner's desires	My partner's regrets

Wish clauses

Function	Rule	Examples
to express desire	Use subjunctive of simple past tense or *might, could, should* + infinitive in clause after *wish*. The use of *that* is optional.	**a.** *I wish (that) I were rich enough to buy my own apartment.* **b.** *We wish (that) we could go back to South America.*
to express regrets	Use past perfect in clause after *wish*. The use of *that* is optional.	*They wish (that) they hadn't left South America.*

D. Read and compare these pairs of sentences. What similarities and differences do you notice in each pair?

1. **(a)** Only in the past 300 years has the idea of a private personal life developed.
   (b) The idea of a private personal life has developed only in the past 300 years.
2. **(a)** Only after he had left home did he realize how much he loved his parents.
   (b) He realized how much he loved his parents only after he had left home.
3. **(a)** Only with the help of their friends and family did the ex-prisoners learn to readjust to life outside prison.
   (b) The ex-prisoners learned to readjust to life outside prison only with the help of their friends and family.

E. Rewrite the following statements giving emphasis to the phrase or clause with *only* and making any necessary changes to the word order and verb forms.

1. She learned to speak Japanese only after she had lived in Japan for many years.
2. I finished decorating my bedroom only after my friends helped me.
3. Christopher Reeve learned to face up to life again only with the support of his family.
4. We realized we had bought the wrong house only after we had lived in it for a year.
5. You can overcome serious problems only if you try hard.

Initial *only* for emphasis

Rule	Examples
Invert the verb and subject of the main verb when the statement begins with a clause or phrase with an initial *only*.	*Only after considerable effort can we learn a foreign language.*
If the main verb phrase does not contain an auxiliary or a modal auxiliary, use *do*.	*Only after he left home **did** he realize how much he loved his parents.*

Test yourself

F. Complete the following text with the correct form and tense of the verbs in parentheses.

Only after they had returned from South America, **(1)** _____ they _____ (realize) how much they had learned from living there. In fact, they wished they **(2)** _____ (stay) longer, as there was still so much to do, see, and learn. However, the companies they worked for insisted that they return to the U.S. Only with considerable difficulty, however, **(3)** _____ they _____ (adjust) to life back in their own country. They missed the warmth of their Latin American friends, the exotic food, and the fabulous scenery. They wish they **(4)** _____ (spend) their next vacation back in South America, but the economic situation is so tough at the moment that this might not be possible. I guess we all wish we **(5)** _____ (go) somewhere exotic for our next vacation, but only if I win the lottery **(6)** _____ this _____ (be) possible.

Echoing to encourage conversation

We can use short "echoing" responses to show that we're listening and to encourage the other person to keep talking.

Echoing words or phrases: That house has six bedrooms. *Six bedrooms?*

I'm thinking about studying Chinese next year. *Chinese?*

I can't understand this book. *You can't?* or *Can't you?*

Short questions: I just got a new apartment. *You did?* or *Did you?*

A. PAIR WORK Where do you live now? What do you like and dislike about your home? If you could change anything about your house or apartment, what would you change? Use responses from the box to encourage your partner to keep talking.

B. PAIR WORK Situation: The government of your city has announced a design contest for "The Ideal Home." New suburbs will be built using the best house design. Design a house or apartment for a family of two adults and two children. Draw a floor plan, which includes the rooms, doors, windows, furniture, and any other details you like. Add labels to explain the features of the house or apartment.

Hang your floor plan on the classroom wall. Take turns with your partner. One person stands next to your floor plan explaining the features of their "Ideal Home," while the other walks around the room looking at other students' work. Then switch roles.

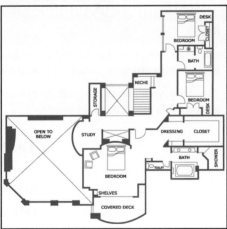

C. What interesting ideas did you hear? Are there houses or apartments that have these features?

According to a University of California study, 78% of people in Hungary own their homes, compared with 66% in the U.S., 53% in the U.K., and only 35% in Sweden.

5 Vocabulary in Detail

A. Study the text to understand the words in **bold**.

While millions of people all over the world are extremely **well-off,** there are many more who are desperately poor. In fact, they are so **hard-up** that they cannot **afford** to meet many of their basic needs. For example, they cannot offer their children any form of education. Instead of going to school, the children have to work alongside their parents **in agriculture** or in the home, or they have to work **in industry** where they are paid **derisory** wages just because they are children. Fortunately, many governments are now **making enormous efforts** not only to reduce **child labor** but also to eradicate all forms of **bad employer practice.** In some countries, for example, children can be employed only if the company for which they work guarantees that they will not work full time and that when they are not working, they will receive a good basic education **at the company's expense.** Other basic needs of people who **live on the breadline** are being met not just through **good employer practices** but with the help of

international aid organizations, such as Habitat for Humanity International, which provides **low-income groups** in both developing and industrialized countries with the opportunity to acquire simple, decent, **affordable** houses. The houses are sold **at cost** and built by the future owners working in **partnership** with teams of international volunteers.

B. PAIR WORK Complete these statements with the correct form of one of the **bolded** words or phrases in A.

1. To be _____ is another way of saying to have very little money.
2. People who _____ barely have enough to eat.
3. People who do not earn very high wages are in _____ groups.
4. You cannot _____ something when you do not have enough money to buy it.
5. Save the Children is an example of an _____.
6. If you sell something without making a profit you sell it _____.
7. When you are _____ with someone, you cooperate with them in a business or to complete a task.
8. If something is _____, you can pay for it without difficulty.
9. Giving workers reasonable rest periods is an example of _____.
10. In most industrialized countries, _____ is illegal but it is still common and even necessary in many developing countries.
11. When people _____, they try very hard to do something.
12. People who do not have to worry about money are _____.

13. A _____ sum of money is very small indeed.
14. If my boss pays for something I do then I do it _____.

C. Circle the correct interpretation of the *idiomatic* expressions in these sentences.

1. *There's no place like home.*
   Home is the best place to be.
   Home is the worst place to be.

2. Look at those two children! They are *getting on like a house on fire.*
   They are getting on very badly.
   They are getting on very well.

3. *Home is where the heart is.*
   Home is alongside the people you love.
   Home is far from the people you love.

4. *I'm feeling homesick.*
   I wish I could get away from home.
   I am missing my home.

5. My best friend's house is *a home away from home* for me.
   I feel just as happy in my friend's house as I do in my own.
   I feel unhappy in my friend's house.

6. That movie with Cruise in it was *nothing to write home about.*
   The movie was very impressive.
   The movie was not very impressive.

Listening
strategy

Noticing opinions and inferences

To understand how someone feels, think about other information beyond just the words they say.

EXAMPLE
Vera: Did you enjoy the movie?
Bob: It was very long.

Notice the *inference* that Bob didn't enjoy the movie, even though he has not said anything directly negative.

Before listening

A. PAIR WORK What are the advantages and disadvantages of renting an apartment as compared to owning a house? Which would you prefer to do?

First listening

B. You will hear a conversation between three family members (a mother, a father, and a daughter) who are looking for a new home. Think about the overall meaning and make inferences about each person's opinion. Write the correct family member next to the opinions. There is one extra space—write *no one* there.

_____ prefers owning a house—because you make all the decisions yourself.

_____ prefers owning a house—because you have more freedom.

_____ prefers renting an apartment—because it's cheaper to live there.

_____ prefers renting an apartment—because a house is too much work.

Second listening

C. Listen again. Write down two details that helped you find the answers in exercise B.

After listening

D. How can the family resolve this issue?

Test yourself

E. Listen to the conversation and answer the question. You will need to make an inference.

What does the man think about the apartment?

a. He wants three bedrooms. **b.** It's too expensive.

c. He'd rather have a house. **d.** It's too small.

Writing a paragraph around a topic sentence

Before you write

A. GROUP WORK Discuss the following questions.

1. What is a paragraph and why do you think a text is normally divided into paragraphs?
2. Approximately how long, in number of words and sentences, do you think a paragraph should be?

B. In the same groups, read the definition of a topic sentence. Decide which of the sentences below are good topic sentences and which are not. Give reasons for your decisions.

> *A* topic sentence expresses the main idea of a paragraph. It creates, in the reader, expectations about the contents of the paragraph. It usually comes early on in the paragraph, but it does not have to be the first sentence. It is followed, or surrounded by, sentences that support the primary idea.

1. My house is small and has a red front door.
2. My house is in a very good location.
3. There are many reasons why the number of homeless people all over the world has increased.
4. A home is a basic human need.
5. The success of that aid organization in helping people meet their basic human needs has been due to several factors.
6. Let me tell you about my dream house.

3. A sturdy Habitat for Humanity International house will considerably ease their worries.
4. When he can leave his crops, he walks long distances to search for building materials.
5. Despite its idyllic location, Papua New Guinea faces tough housing challenges.
6. Eku and his wife, Gemisa, are in their fifties and the prospect of continually rebuilding is a source of anxiety as they grow older and resources become more scarce.

C. PAIR WORK Read the following sentences. Identify the topic sentence, the supporting sentences, and a suitable concluding sentence. Then work in pairs and compare your answers. Once you have agreed, decide on the order of the sentences and write them out as a complete paragraph.

1. For Eku Jacob, a subsistence farmer, gathering the timber and grass for his house is a never-ending task.
2. Natural materials are difficult to gather and a tropical climate wreaks havoc on traditionally built shelters.

Write

D. GROUP WORK Form groups again. Choose one of the topic sentences from exercise B above and use it as the primary idea to write a paragraph of at least five sentences. Before you start writing, decide whether your paragraph is to be mostly narrative, expository, or descriptive. Then join up with another group. Read and comment on their paragraphs. Think about how successfully the topic sentence has been supported in the other sentences.

A. PAIR WORK Read the following situation and roles. Decide which role you are going to have and take five minutes to prepare it. Act out the role play. Then change roles with your partner. Take a few more minutes to prepare your new role. Act out the role play again.

Situation: An interview with a homeless person in your country.

Role 1:
You are a reporter for a national newspaper, and you are going to write an article about the causes of homelessness in your capital city. You are going to interview a homeless person. Prepare to ask questions about why the person became homeless, how he or she spends his or her time, and how he or she would like to see the problem of homelessness in your country solved.

Role 2:
You are a homeless person in your capital city. A newspaper reporter is going to ask you about your life as a homeless person. Prepare to answer questions about why you became homeless, how you spend your day, and how you would like the problem of the homeless to be solved.

B. GROUP WORK Working alone, check (✓) the items in the list that you consider are basic human necessities and put an *X* by the ones you think are luxuries. Then work with a partner and try to reach an agreement about all the items. Join up with another pair to see if you all agree. Discuss your group's decisions with the class.

a. basic, decent, affordable dwelling _____
b. free access to the Internet _____
c. free healthcare _____
d. free primary, secondary, and college education _____
e. inexpensive and efficient public transportation _____
f. free access to museums and art galleries _____
g. subsidized gas for private cars _____
h. free access to gyms and swimming pools _____

C. CLASS TASK Debate the following topic: Technological innovations such as TV, computers, and the Internet have greatly contributed to destroying people's sense of "home."

For more detail about Home, view the CNN video. Activities to accompany the video begin on page 137.

Survivors

Communication

Describing animal characteristics and behavior

Discussing human survival traits and strategies

Talking about a scenario

Grammar

Subject and object complements

Infinitives of purpose in initial position

Vocabulary

Review of climate lexis

Climatic extremes

Climate-related idioms

Skills

Scanning a biology text and making detailed notes

Listening and finding supporting details

Writing: structuring a narrative paragraph

1 Warm Up

A. With the class, describe the pictures and discuss why these people and animals are able to survive.

B. PAIR WORK Make statements about the animals in the box using the words below. Then, with another pair, brainstorm for all the other information you know about these living things and share this information with the class.

EXAMPLE: *Camels are pack animals that live and work in the desert.*

wild	insects	in a nest
domestic	species	in fields
pet	reptiles	in the mountains
endangered	animals	in a den
small		in the desert
hard-working		in the ocean
predatory		in the jungle
pack		in the arctic
farm		in a house
		in yards

camels	bees lions	cows
snakes	polar bears	dogs
whales	elephants	llamas
birds	crocodiles	

C. GROUP WORK Talk about the animals and insects in the box. Discuss which ones are most common in your country and what importance they have.

Reading strategy

Looking for cognates

In scientific texts, many technical terms are derived from Latin and Greek. These words are often universal, so you should be able to recognize them easily.

Before you read

A. With the class, brainstorm and list all the things you know about these insects and discuss their similarities and differences.

bee

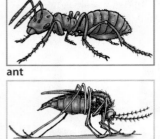
ant

mosquito

centipede

First reading

B. Scan the text and decide if the statements are True *(T)* or False *(F)*. Identify the parts of the text that support the true statement and correct the false ones.

a. Many kinds of animals and insects can survive in desert temperatures of 70° C. __

b. Spiders and centipedes eat silver desert ants. __

c. Unlike humans and insects, some bacteria can survive in temperatures of 1,000° C. __

d. Desert ants can survive in temperatures of 66° C because they move so fast their feet barely touch the sand. __

e. Human legs work just as fast as the legs of the silver desert ant. __

Feel the Heat

1. On a blisteringly sunny day in the Sahara, surface temperatures can peak above 70° C. This is more than hot—the searing air makes breathing very difficult, and the sand is not only too hot to touch with naked° skin, it
5 can even burn. In this environment, most animals, including humans, would be dead in a matter of minutes, because anything warm-blooded falls prey to dehydration° and thermal shock. Even camels can find the going very tough. But if you look closely, you will
10 see tiny holes in the sand. When the sun is at its height, the toughest insects on earth emerge° to forage for food in the sweltering surroundings usually for no more than a few minutes at a time.
2. This is the domain° of the silver desert ant
15 *(Cataglyphis bombycina)*, one of the most resilient creatures on earth. It doesn't just survive in this heat; it positively thrives,° using it as a defense against less hardy predators. To do this, the silver ant has evolved an extreme lifestyle with long periods of inactivity every

20 day, combined with a frantic dash° for food as the temperature rockets. Its sources of food are those killed or wounded by the heat—spiders, centipedes, and other insects. To collect their meat, the ants explode from their nest only when the temperature is unbearable for
25 most other animals. Once they're on the surface, they swarm° around for between eight and ten minutes looking for the remains of heat-struck victims. Once the temperature has climbed into the zone that not even they can survive, the ants scurry home, lugging° any
30 food back to the nest. As temperatures fall later on, the cycle is repeated. And that's it—for an entire day.
3. It's a gruesome,° edgy existence. But it's also a fine example of how evolutionary pressure can create adaptations that work successfully in an otherwise
35 inhospitable place. An internal temperature of 50° C is around the maximum possible for a complex active organism. Beyond this, the biochemical processes that make life possible start to fall apart. Respiration becomes difficult and oxygen can no longer be carried
40 around the body effectively. The brain and nervous

system also start to degrade. Bacteria rely on simpler processes, and some will still be going strong at 1,000° C. But for insects and all other forms of life, nature has yet to find a way to cross the 50° C limit.

45 **4.** So how can ants survive in ambient temperatures of 65° C and more? To make life possible, desert ants rely on some ingenious evolutionary adaptations. The simplest are their long legs and small feet, allowing them to skip across the surface, reducing contact with the 50 scorching sand and rock. A few millimeters above the earth, the temperature can be six to seven degrees cooler. Flat on the sand these ants wouldn't stand a chance. But by perching above it, they limit the amount of heat picked up from the ground. Any thermal input comes 55 mostly from the surrounding air.

5. They also move fast. If you've ever stuck your hand out of the car window on a sweltering day, you'll know the strong flow of air can have an obvious cooling effect, even if the air itself is pretty warm. To make the most of 60 air cooling and also to avoid predators, desert ants speed from place to place at more than one meter per second.

At around half the speed of a walking human, this may not sound like much, but it's close to a record for insects. And it's worth remembering that while we can 65 cover a lot of ground with a single stride, ant legs are much shorter and have to work a lot faster to keep up a comparable pace. If human legs worked that fast, we'd be approaching the sound barrier each time we stepped out through the front door! (*Focus:* "Discover the 70 world around you," March 2002, pages 35-37. www.focusmag.co.uk)

---

naked = without clothes
dehydration = serious loss of body water
emerge = come out
domain = land occupied, controlled by
thrive = grow strong and healthy
dash = rush
swarm = move in large groups close together as one body
lug = carry a heavy burden with difficulty
gruesome = horrifying

Vocabulary in context

C. Complete the sentences with words from the text.

1. In P.1, line 1, *blistering* has a similar meaning to (a) _____ in P1, line 3.
   (b) _____ in P1, line 12.
   (c) _____ in P4, line 50.

2. _____ in P1, line 7 means "become a victim of."

3. _____ in P1, line 8 means "heat-related" or "heat-induced."

4. _____ in P1, line 11 means "work hard to find something."

5. *Hardy* in P2, line 18 has a similar meaning to _____ in P2, line 15.

6. _____ in P2, line 29 means "run quickly in all directions."

7. _____ in P3, line 32 means "nervous or stressful."

8. *Fall apart* in P3, line 38 has a similar meaning to _____ in P3, line 41.

9. _____ in P4, line 53 means "stay in a high position."

10. _____ in P5, line 65 means "a long step."

Second reading

D. Read the text again. Then work in pairs to complete the missing headings and details in these outline notes.

1. **Conditions in the Sahara in which silver desert ants survive**
   a. Blisteringly sunny
   b. _____
   c. _____ so it can burn naked skin
   d. _____ so even camels find it hard to survive

2. **Method** _____
   a. Dash out for food when temperatures rise
   b. Look for _____
   c. _____
   d. Rush back to the nest with food when _____

3. **Reasons why most organisms die at internal temperatures of 50° C**
   a. _____   **b.** _____

4. **Reasons why** _____
   a. Have developed ingenious evolutionary adaptations, e.g., _____
   b. _____, e.g., at more than one meter per second

Discussion

E. With the class, discuss how desert ants survive in the Sahara. Then give other examples of adaptation to an environment.

Subject and object complements

Infinitives of purpose in initial position

Practice

A. PAIR WORK Match the description of the subject complements in the box on the right with the bolded complements in these statements.

| noun phrase | infinitive phrase | noun clause | adjective or adjectives |

1. The silver desert ant looks **small and weak.**
2. The silver desert ant is **an intelligent insect.**
3. In the desert temperatures of 50° C, respiration becomes **difficult.**
4. The ant's objective is **to find some food** as quickly as possible.
5. Speed **is what helps the ant to survive in the blistering heat.**

B. Complete the sentences below with the information in the box.

| to go walking in the Gobi desert | the secret to | blistering hot | corpses | what makes breathing |

1. The desert looks ____ in these pictures.
2. My plan for when I retire is _____.
3. Walking very slowly in the desert is _____easier.
4. At 50° C, most healthy living organisms become _____.
5. Fitness is _____ survival in extreme climatic conditions.

C. PAIR WORK Match the type of object complements in the box with the bolded complements in the sentences below.

| a noun or a noun phrase | an adjective or adjectives |

1. Many people find desert travel **horrifying and dangerous.**
2. Others regard desert travel as **a wonderful adventure.**
3. Some even consider desert travel **romantic.**
4. Most normal people recognize a beach holiday **as the ideal way** to relax.
5. That travel agent took me for **a real fool** and tried to convince me to go on a really expensive desert trip.

Interact

D. Complete the statements. Then work with a partner and ask each other about your opinions. Use the information to tell the class what you have learned about your partner.

EXAMPLE:
S1: What do you regard as the most difficult aspect of learning a foreign language?
S2: Listening. And what about you?

1. I regard _listening_ as the most difficult aspect of learning a foreign language.
2. I recognize _____ as the greatest singer who has ever lived.
3. I find _____ a really easy sport because I played it a lot when I was a child.
4. I consider _____ the most wonderful time of the year.
5. I would describe _____ as the most exciting thing I have ever done.

E. Match the infinitives of purpose on the right with the incomplete statements on the left.

1. _____ desert ants leave their nests when temperatures sky rocket.
2. _____ these high temperatures, the desert ant relies on some ingenious evolutionary adaptations.
3. _____ many people have to do two jobs.
4. _____ people with decent houses, Habitat sells their houses at cost price.
5. _____ depression, Christopher Reeve established a medical research foundation.

a. To overcome
b. To resist
c. To provide
d. To collect food
e. To earn a living

F. PAIR WORK Complete these statements with true information about yourself. Then work with a partner and exchange your information.

1. To relax after a hard day's work, I _____
2. To earn a decent living, I have to _____
3. To resist treats like chocolates and cakes, I _____
4. To try and learn English words, I _____
5. To overcome sadness, I _____

FYI

To emphasize a reason or purpose, place an infinitive at the beginning of a sentence.

EXAMPLE:
To overcome the problem, she started exercising.

Rules and notes	Examples
Subject complements	
A subject complement describes the subject.	_1. Paul looks hot and bothered._
An intransitive verb links the subject and its complement.	_2. Deserts are dangerous places._
A subject complement can be an adjective (1), a noun phrase (2), an infinitive phrase (3), or a noun clause (4).	_3. My plan is to retire at fifty and spend the rest of my life relaxing._
	4. Beach holidays are what I dream about.
Object complements	
An object complement describes the direct object, which can be either a noun (1) or a pronoun (2).	_1. Many people find winter depressing._
An object complement can be either a noun (2) or an adjective (1).	_2. That guy took me for the boss._
Verbs such as consider, find, and prove take a noun or adjective complement (3). A few verbs are followed by as or for and an object complement: regard as, accept as, describe as, mistake for, and take for (4).	_3. I consider it a mistake._ _She finds him very entertaining._
	4. I would describe him as quite funny.

Test yourself

G. Fill in the blanks in the text with a suitable word or expression.

a depressing season
to overcome
to cool off
for natural light
ideal
the perfect solution
hopeless

(1) _____ on a hot summer's day, most people find drinking ice-cold drinks **(2)** _____. In contrast, in winter they regard hot, spicy beverages as **(3)** _____ because they help them resist colds and other winter illnesses. Some people consider winter **(4)** _____, because it is so dark. **(5)** _____ their winter blues, doctors recommend they get lots of light, even artificial light. Apparently, the human body mistakes light from a lamp **(6)** _____ so the artificial light has just as good an effect on a person's mood as sunlight.

Speaking focus

Talking about a scenario

Sometimes in a discussion or presentation, you want your listeners to think about a situation. You can use these expressions.

Suppose your car breaks down in the desert. *Imagine that* there is an earthquake. *What if* you get lost?

FYI scenario = a situation that could possibly happen but has not happened yet

A. PAIR WORK Look at the box below. Which three items are the most important to take with you when you go on vacation? Tell your partner, and explain scenarios when they would be useful.

matches   a compass   a pocket knife   bandages   a cell phone plastic bags   a small radio   a list of doctors' telephone numbers a flashlight   aspirin

B. GROUP WORK Situation: Your sports club wants to send a team to a five-day adventure race in a rain forest in Africa. In the race, teams will travel by running, swimming, mountain biking, rafting, and horseback riding and the whole team must finish together. Read the information about these people and choose four members for the team, including at least one woman. (You can also choose students in your class!) Then take turns explaining your decisions and reasons to the class. Use the expressions you have learned to talk about possible scenarios.

C. Would you like to take part in an adventure race. Why or why not?

Name: Richard   **Age:** 47

Occupation: Army officer

Experience: Worked for twelve years in the desert. Lifts weights and runs twelve kilometers every day.

Name: Sharon   **Age:** 28

Occupation: Police officer

Experience: Saved four people from a burning car last year. Likes biking and rafting.

Name: Dave   **Age:** 19

Occupation: Student

Experience: National swimming champion. Has never played a team sport.

Name: Peter   **Age:** 29

Occupation: International tour guide

Experience: Speaks five languages. Good at running and swimming, but afraid of horses.

Name: Tania   **Age:** 34

Occupation: Doctor

Experience: Doesn t like most sports only biking. Has won many cycling events.

Name: Lisa   **Age:** 26

Occupation: Horseback riding teacher

Experience: Did volunteer work in Africa for two years. Plays basketball and tennis.

Adventure racing is a new sport in which teams of four men and women race across long distances in difficult environments, twenty-four hours a day. In the Eco-Challenge, a famous adventure race, teams race 500 kilometers in ten days. They travel by running, climbing ropes, kayaking, mountain biking, and horseback riding. To win the race, all team members must finish together, so cooperation is very important. Every year, the race is held in a different country and in a different setting, like the jungles of Malaysia, the desert of Morocco, or the mountains of Canada.

A. wind snow rain sun frost cloud fog storm ice winter

B. hot chilly freezing mild cold sizzling warm cool

A. With the class, brainstorm for adjectives derived from the words in box A. Use each one to make a sentence. Then write the words from box B next to the corresponding temperature on the thermometer.

B. PAIR WORK Match the groups of adjectives on the left with the nouns on the right and try to use them together in sentences.

1. light, strong, icy   **a.** storm
2. severe, tropical   **b.** rain
3. bright, gentle, warm   **c.** fog
4. light, heavy, torrential **d.** wind
5. dense, thick, patchy   **e.** sunshine

C. Study the text to understand the meanings of the words in **bold**.

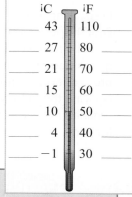

iC		iF	
___ 43		110 ___	
___ 27		80 ___	
___ 21		70 ___	
___ 15		60 ___	
___ 10		50 ___	
___ 4		40 ___	
___ −1		30 ___	

Many people, when traveling in Southeast Asia, try to avoid the **monsoon** season—between April and October—as it is much harder to travel around. Also, mosquitoes are common at this time of year, making travel even more **hazardous.**

In the northern hemisphere, typically between January and March, **blizzards** can **bring life to a standstill.** Drivers either cannot see through the fast-falling snow or their vehicles simply **get stuck** in deep **snowdrifts.** Even when the **thaw** comes, things don't necessarily improve, as the melted snow can sometimes cause severe **flooding.**

Some parts of the world, especially islands in temperate zones, do not experience climatic extremes, but there can be certain disadvantages to temperate climates. Because it is often **overcast,** it can be rather **gloomy,** and some people can suffer because of the shortage of sunlight. In summer, the sun is sometimes hidden behind a layer of clouds making the atmosphere very **muggy.** Even in summer, the rain is often not far away, though it may only be a mild **drizzle.**

D. Match these meanings with the **bolded** words in exercise C.

1. rather dark _____
2. heavy tropical rainstorm _____
3. very dangerous _____
4. heavy snowstorm _____
5. make everything stop _____
6. light rain _____

7. warm and humid _____
8. piles of snow _____
9. cloudy _____
10. be unable to move _____
11. covering of land with water _____
12. melting of ice or snow _____

E. Circle the correct interpretation of the *idioms* and *metaphors* in these sentences.

1. He's *in a gloomy mood.*
   He's feeling really optimistic.
   He's feeling rather pessimistic.
2. There has been *a thaw in the tension* between them.
   The tension is increasing.
   The tension is decreasing.
3. He *stormed out* of the room when he heard the news.
   He went out quietly.
   He went out angrily.

Listening
strategy

Finding supporting details

In speaking, as in writing, English speakers often state their main idea and then give supporting details to prove or explain this point. Noticing this helps you to organize notes while listening.

Before you listen

A. Who was the first person to climb Mount Everest? The first person to travel in space? The first person to reach the South Pole? Who are some other famous explorers? What are the most difficult places on earth to travel to?

First listening

B. You are going to listen to a radio interview about Fridtjof Nansen, an important explorer. Listen and find this information.

Where he was born:_____ When he was born: _____

The part of the world he explored: _____

Two expeditions he made: 1. _____ 2. _____

Second listening

C. Listen again and take notes about these parts of the interview. The main ideas are given. Write the details that the speaker gives to explain the main idea.

Nansen was a hero because:

1. He showed great courage. _____

2. He was a great leader. _____

His work was important because:

1. He developed a new way to travel. _____

2. He made important scientific discoveries. _____

After listening

D. Which is the most difficult environment to survive in—a desert, mountains, a rain forest, the polar regions? Why?

Test yourself

E. Listen to the talk about "Clothes for Survival in Cold Weather" and take notes about the supporting details. Then listen to the questions and circle the answers.

1. a. a hat   **b.** boots   **c.** a plastic sheet   **d.** a heavy coat

2. a. a jacket   **b.** plastic bags   **c.** boots   **d.** an umbrella

Structuring a narrative paragraph

Before you write

A. GROUP WORK First check that you know the meanings of all of the following words and expressions. Then use them to speculate about and discuss what you think happened to Bangau.

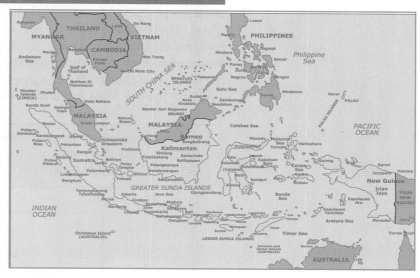

Bangau's Survival

Bangau Samuel	all of the remaining passengers	to Jakarta
a plane crash	survived	lucky
a young Indonesian man	Indonesian jungle	called
from Tarakan	with his father	died

B. In the same groups, read the paragraph about Bangau's survival and choose, from this list, the most suitable topic sentence for the paragraph. If necessary, reread the definition of a good topic sentence on page 19.

1. Bangau Samuel is a 20-year-old Indonesian high school student.
2. Bangau Samuel considers himself one of the luckiest young men in the world.
3. When Bangau Samuel goes to university he wants to study to be a teacher.
4. Bangau Samuel and his father traveled together a lot.
5. Bangau Samuel's mother could not believe the news of his survival.

When he woke up lying on the ground a week ago, Bangau had no idea where he was. He was surrounded by thick vegetation, but through the treetops, he could see a clear blue sky. He got to his feet and looked around him. There were dead bodies everywhere and bits and pieces of a light plane were dangling from the trees or scattered on the ground. Then he remembered. He had fallen asleep on a flight from Tarakan to Jakarta—with his father, who was traveling with him by his side. The plane must have crashed and he was clearly the only survivor. He set off through the jungle to look for help. Two days later, when he was still struggling alone through the jungle, rescue workers reached the plane. The crew and all the passengers were declared dead so no one went to look for Bangau. In fact, a day later Bangau's mother buried her husband and what she believed to be Bangau's body. Fortunately, Bangau understood the forest and kept walking downhill in the direction of flat land. Six days after the crash, he walked into the rice fields of a local farmer, who immediately took care of him and arranged for him to be reunited with his mother.

Write

C. Read the story of Bangau's survival again and decide whether the supporting sentences for the topic sentence you chose are mostly (a) descriptive, (b) expository, or (c) narrative. Then either invent a story of survival or use a real survival story that you know about and write a paragraph, narrating the main details. Don't forget to begin with a topic sentence which creates expectations in your reader.

A. GROUP WORK Prepare a description to be given orally of the kinds of conditions you would expect to experience in a jungle. Think about the climatic conditions, the vegetation, and the animal and insect life. Then working in the same pairs, decide which five of the items in the box you consider essential if you were going to survive for a week in the jungle with a guide who knew the jungle well. Then join up with two other students and compare your choices. Try to agree about the items. With the whole class, agree on the five most popular items.

cell phone   personal stereo   hammock   insect repellent   sleeping pills
compass   stomach medicine   torch water   sterilizing tablets
cans of food   box of matches or lighter   good book

B. PAIR WORK List at least five personal traits that you believe help people survive life's challenges and difficulties. How do these traits help people survive? Put a check (✓) against the traits that you yourself have and an *X* against the ones you don't have. Opposite to each item on the list, write examples of the kinds of things that are easy, difficult, or impossible for you to do as a result of the trait. Then work with a classmate you know well and talk to each other about the things in life you find easy, difficult, or impossible and explain how these are affected by your personal traits. Tell the class something new you have learned about your classmate.

C. CLASS TASK Organize a debate on this topic: Human beings may not survive beyond this century.

For more detail about Survivors, view the CNN video. Activities to accompany the video begin on page 138.

Review Unit 1

Review Your Grammar

A. Circle the word or words in parentheses that can correctly complete each sentence.

1. I wish that I (have / had / have had) a pet.
2. My friend Al wishes that he (went / could go / had gone) to China next year.
3. My brother wishes that he (live / would live / had lived) in the 1800s.
4. The patient wishes that the doctor (comes / would come / had come) soon.
5. The movie star wishes that she (isn't / weren't / couldn't be) so famous.
6. The bird wishes that the cat (would go away / goes away / will go away).

B. Complete each sentence using words from the box. Add *as* and *for* when necessary.

> very talented   a homemaker   a highly successful politician   adventurous people
> to get home right away   what you're thinking

1. I have been traveling for six weeks and now my plan is _____.
2. In Hollywood, that new movie star is regarded _____.
3. War correspondents are usually _____.
4. Sometimes people think they know _____.
5. People know Ms. Reese because she is a famous writer, but she is also described _____.
6. Because Ms. Reese was wearing jeans and a T-shirt, I mistook her _____.

High Challenge

C. Write the letter of the correct word or phrase in the blank.

1. _____ from an illness, it may be necessary to take some medicine.
   a. His recovering **b.** Recovered **c.** Recover **d.** To recover
2. _____ did they miss their little dog.
   a. After he died only **b.** After he only died **c.** Only after he died
   d. After he only died
3. I wish that I _____ German.
   a. can speak **b.** could speak **c.** would speak **d.** was speaking
4. Liang _____ in Singapore for three years when she got a surprising letter.
   a. had been living **b.** has been living **c.** lived **d.** lives
5. Only on Sundays _____ without paying.
   a. they could visit the museum **b.** you can visit the museum
   c. can you visit the museum **d.** we will visit the museum
6. We wish that we _____ more when we were in high school.
   a. study **b.** were studying **c.** studied **d.** had studied

FYI

Knowing a word is complex. Some elements you may need to know are: understanding the word when it is written or spoken, recalling it when you need it, using it grammatically, and spelling it correctly. When you find a new word, it is helpful to ask yourself, "Will I need to use this word when I am writing or speaking, or do I only need to understand it when I hear it or read it?"

Review Your Vocabulary

A. Match the opposites.

___ **1.** healthy	**a.** sick
___ **2.** well organized	**b.** confident
___ **3.** insecure	**c.** in a hurry
___ **4.** wise	**d.** stupid
___ **5.** patient	**e.** not carefully planned

B. Use words from the box to complete the conversation.

> fighting a losing battle   relaxing   emerging   feeling   breaking up with
> falling prey to   thriving   giving up hope

Rita: I am **(1)** _____ so homesick!
Ben: What's the matter? Are you **(2)** _____ some gloomy thoughts?
Rita: Not really. But I'm **(3)** _____ my old boyfriend and it's not so easy.
Ben: You're not **(4)** _____, are you?
Rita: No, I guess not. But yesterday our romance was **(5)** _____ and to-day it seems to be finished. I feel like I'm **(6)** _____ with my feel-ings.
Ben: How about **(7)** _____ for a while? It'll probably make you feel bet-ter. You could spend a weekend at a spa.
Rita: That's not a bad idea. Maybe it'll help me start **(8)** _____ from my depression.

C. Match each statement with the correct echoing response.

___ **1.** It hasn't stopped raining for three whole days!	**a.** It isn't?
___ **2.** The sun came out yesterday for a few minutes.	**b.** It did?
___ **3.** The soccer players don't like this weather.	**c.** Are they?
___ **4.** They won't be able to practice this afternoon.	**d.** Hasn't it?
___ **5.** It isn't going to rain tomorrow.	**e.** Don't they?
___ **6.** All the teams are going to practice tomorrow.	**f.** They won't?

Review Your Speaking

Fluency

A. Make notes below about some adversity that you or someone else has had to overcome. Then tell a partner or a small group about the situation. Answer any questions they may have.

The problem _____	
Solutions that worked	**Why they worked**
_____	_____
_____	_____
Solutions that didn't work	**Why they didn't work**
_____	_____
_____	_____
_____	_____

B. PAIR WORK Choose a photo and take turns describing the person in the photo to your partner. Then discuss how the two people in the photos are alike and how they differ.

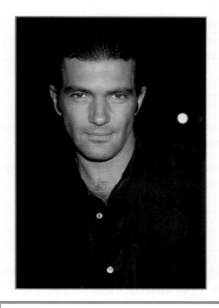 

F•A•Q

Why do oral tests use photos?

The first part of many oral tests involves describing or comparing photos. Photos are also used to introduce a theme for conversation. Having a concrete task such as describing a photo is a way to help you focus. It gives you something to start talking about. To practice, you should try describing and comparing many different kinds of photos.

Review Your Listening

A. GROUP WORK When you were a small child before you started school, who took care of you? Was this a good arrangement? In your country today, who takes care of small children if both their parents have jobs? What kind of care is best for children?

Listening 1

B. You are going to hear two speakers talking about how the government should help families with small children. Listen to the first speaker. In her opinion, who should take care of small children? Why?

C. Listen again and take notes on two things the government should do.

1. _____

2. _____

D. Check the statements that this speaker would probably agree with. You will need to make inferences.

_____ Parents are much more important than teachers in a child's life.

_____ The government can also help families by starting more childcare centers.

_____ The first few years are the most important time in a child's life.

_____ Mothers shouldn't have jobs until their children start school.

_____ Fathers are not as important as mothers in caring for a child.

Listening 2

E. Now listen to the second speaker. In his opinion, who should take care of children? Why?

F. Listen again and take notes on three things this speaker says the government should do.

1. _____

2. _____

3. _____

G. Check the statements that this speaker would probably agree with. You will need to make inferences.

_____ Young children can learn important things from teachers.

_____ Childcare is not an easy job.

_____ Most working mothers get jobs for selfish reasons.

_____ Young children need to have their mother at home with them.

_____ Women do some very important jobs in this country.

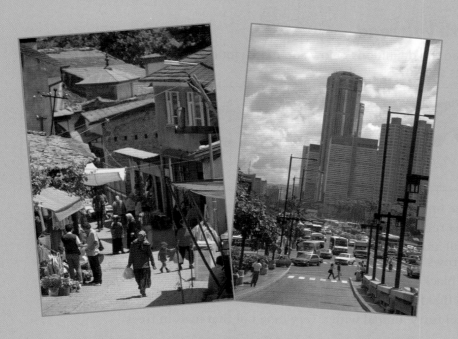

Progress

Communication

Discussing rural and urban lifestyles

Debating industrialization and global warming

Leading a discussion

Grammar

Relative adverbs + clause

Omission of the head noun or the relative adverb

Vocabulary

Review of geographical features

Fauna and conservation

Skills

Skimming for main topic areas and making detailed notes

Listening for and finding a time sequence

Writing an expository paragraph

1 Warm Up

A. Look at the pictures. Describe each place and discuss the similarities and differences between them. Speculate about why each place is so different.

B. PAIR WORK Classify the words in the box under the headings below.

High areas of land or sand	Low/flat/deep land or sand	Places with water

waterfall   dune   river   ocean   valley   hill   lake   stream   canyon mountain   plain   sea

Use the words above and other words you know with the adjectives below to produce as many sentences as you can.

winding   high   deep   flat   shallow   steep   rocky   straight   low grassy   hilly

EXAMPLE: *When we reached the top of the high dune, we saw a flat, grassy plain below us.*

C. Discuss the reasons why some people prefer to live close to nature while others prefer to live in a big city.

Before you read

A. Read the definitions below and match four of the definitions with the pictures shown.

a. 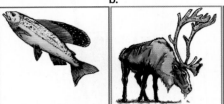 b. c.  d.

1. large furry animal that spends the winter in a cave
2. large reindeer that lives only in North America
3. small animal with large ears; can be a wild animal or a pet; lives in burrows under the ground
4. big black bird that has a very loud cry
5. fish that lives in fresh water
6. small furry animal with a very long tail that lives in trees

Reading strategy

Identifying the writer's point of view

As you read a text, try to discover how the writer feels about the topic. Think carefully about the examples chosen and the sources quoted, as these have been selected to support the writer's particular point of view.

First reading

B. Skim the text and choose a suitable title from the list.

a. The Advantages of Modernization for Arctic Village
b. The Origins and Future Prospects of Arctic Village
c. The Arctic Village People and their Customs
d. The Life of Animals in and around Arctic Village
e. The Effects of Global Warming on Arctic Village

As a child, Sarah James and her seven brothers and sisters learned how to **snare** rabbits and fish for grayling in the **wilderness** around Arctic Village, a tiny **settlement** of 150 Native Alaskans inside the Arctic Circle. Her brothers and her father hunted caribou, her
5 mother **tanned** the hides° and sewed the fur, and their way of life seemed to reflect the name of their tribe,° Gwich'in, the Land Where Life Begins. Now that feeling of romantic permanence is over. "We used to have four healthy seasons, but all that is **off-balance** now," says
10 Sarah, now 56. "The tree line has changed, the lakes have dried up. Global warming is very real up here."

Since the late 19th century, Arctic Village has been the focal point of the Gwich'in, who **comprise** seven thousand people spread over fifteen villages, still
15 speaking their own language and living in the traditional way by hunting and fishing. The village is reachable only by a ninety-minute flight from Fairbanks, in the center of Alaska. It experiences the extremes of summer when it never darkens and **bitter** winters when it is light for only
20 three hours a day. It straddles two worlds: Arctic Village has satellite television and access to the Internet, but no running water or inside toilets. It has its own post office with the American flag flying beside it, but its traditions owe more to native Alaskan ways, which
25 many in the village see threatened by the desire of the U.S. to drill for oil in the Arctic Refuge immediately to the north of the village.

A more immediate threat, however, comes from the effects of climate change, which are more apparent
30 here than anywhere else in the U.S. So great are the local fears that they called a tribal **gathering** last month for the first time in thirteen years. During it, they blessed° the new solar panels on the roof of their "washeteria," where they do their laundry and take
35 their showers. The panels provide energy in summer and are a reminder of the renewable forms of energy the world has barely explored. But it is the effects of the rise in winter temperatures that the older people in the village worry about. "It used always to be −51° C
40 in the winter but we don't get that anymore," said Kias Peter, seventy-two, one of the village **elders.** "We have lost thirteen lakes around here." And Calvin Tritt, fifty, a former Gwich'in chief added, "The caribou used to have about two inches of fat on them, now they're
45 **scrawny** and they're going loco."°

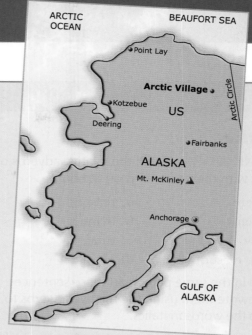

Faith Gemmill, a young member of the Gwich'in steering committee, a body which guides the community in its decision-making, said: "Our people noticed changes about five years ago. Now, our creeks, our lakes,
50 and rivers are drying up. All my life when we went up on the mountain, we would camp by fresh mountain water, and that has gone. There were always ground squirrels, and they have gone too. On the mountains we usually don't run into grizzlies, but last year our hunters came
55 across three different bears. The bears weren't frightened and they tried to attack, so the hunters had to kill them. And the reason why the bears weren't afraid was that they were starving."

The evidence for global warming across Alaska is
60 stark. The average temperature has risen between 3° C and 4.5° C in winter, ten times the rate elsewhere in the world. The tundra has turned from spongy° to dry and many native plants have simply disappeared. The region's polar bears have lost 20% of their weight in the past few
65 years. Recently, a visiting academic asked the Gwich'in in Arctic Village whether they would like to be joined by road to the rest of Alaska. Almost unanimously° the villagers said no. Looking at the miles of rolling mountains and wilderness, disturbed only by the
70 occasional **crack** of a hunting rifle° or **flock** of noisy crows, it is easy to understand why.

(Abridged from *The Guardian*, Monday, July 16 2001, International news page 1.)

hide = tough skin of an animal
tribe = group of people who live in same place and have lots of relatives in the group
bless = ask for God's goodness
loco = crazy
spongy = wet, moist
unanimously = in complete agreement
rifle = gun with a long barrel

Second reading
Vocabulary in context

C. Read the text again and match each definition with one of the **bolded** words in the text.

1. senior citizens who take responsibility for decisions in a community _____
2. group of birds, chickens, sheep, or goats _____
3. icy cold _____
4. catch in a trap _____
5. extremely thin _____
6. sudden very loud noise _____
7. include _____
8. area of land in its natural state, unspoiled by humans _____
9. meeting _____
10. beginnings of a town with very few inhabitants _____
11. not normal _____
12. preserved leather _____

D. Read the story again and decide which of the headings would be suitable for outline notes for the reading text. After selecting the headings, copy them and complete the headings by adding appropriate notes.

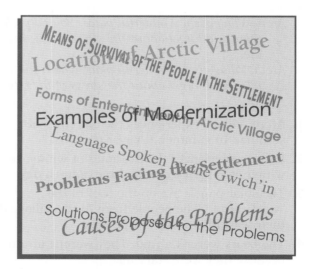

Discussion

E. With the class, discuss all the aspects of life in Arctic Village you would enjoy and all those you would dislike very much. Give your reasons.

Relative adverbs

Practice

A. PAIR WORK Match the relative adverbs on the left with their meanings on the right.

1. where   **a.** reason
2. when   **b.** manner
3. how   **c.** time
4. (the reason) why **d.** place

B. Still in the same pairs, read these sentences. Then rewrite them using the relative adverbs to replace the words in italics.

1. Summer in Alaska is the time *during which* the days are long and the nights short.
2. A settlement is a place *in which* not many people live.
3. The effects of global warming are the reason *for which* the Gwich'in are worried.
4. They have no idea *in what way* they will survive if global warming continues.
5. They dread the day *in which* there will be no caribou or rabbits for them to hunt.

C. Combine the pairs of sentences using one of the adverbs from exercise A and making any necessary deletions. In some cases, there may be two possibilities.

EXAMPLE:
> *Arctic Village is a wonderful place. You can relax there and forget about the stress of big city life.*
> *Arctic Village is a wonderful place where you can relax and forget about the stress of big city life.*

1. Arctic Village experiences the extremes of summer. In summer, it never darkens.
2. It also experiences the extremes of winter. In winter, it is light for only three hours a day.
3. The solar panels are on the roof of the "washeteria." The people from Arctic Village do their washing in the "washeteria."
4. The bears weren't afraid. They weren't afraid because they were starving.
5. All my life we went up on the mountains. We would camp by fresh water.
6. The wilderness is a wide open space. You can be very close to nature there.

7. The people in Arctic Village are happy. They are happy because they live close to nature.
8. The people of Arctic Village will never forget. Their rivers and lakes were full of fish.

Interact

D. Complete the statements with true information about yourself. Then work in pairs and share the information. Tell the class what you have learned about your partner.

1. I need to find out the date (day, year, century, etc.) when _____.
2. I must find out the place (town, city, country, etc.) where _____.
3. I am interested in finding out how _____.
4. I cannot imagine the reason why _____.

E. Work in groups and match the *time periods, places, reasons,* and *processes* in the column on the left with the events and statements on the right. When matching places and events, or times and events, try to use *head words* which are more specific than "place" or "time."

EXAMPLE:
> *Alaska / you can still see a lot of bears and caribou*
> *Alaska is the state where you can still see a lot of bears and caribou.*

1. not eating fatty foods and doing yoga
2. Memphis, Tennessee
3. Korea and Japan
4. learning to speak English well
5. spring
6. a love of special effects
7. 1945
8. a fear of flying

a. World War II ended
b. people fall in love
c. many people do not travel
d. I stay healthy
e. the 2002 World Cup took place
f. you will progress in your profession
g. Elvis Presley was born
h. many people go to modern movies

F. Decide whether the head noun (e.g., place, time, reason) or the relative adverb has been omitted in these sentences.

1. Seoul is where you can see a lot of bridges.
2. Midday is the time the desert ant starts looking for food.
3. Global warming is the reason so many lakes have disappeared in Alaska.
4. The lack of a caring family and a good home in childhood is why some young adults turn to crime.
5. A month or so after his accident is when Christopher Reeve was at his lowest.

Relative adverbs + clause
Omission of the head noun or relative adverb

Pattern + examples	Explanation
Head noun + relative adverb + clause	Use this pattern:
a. *The desert is the place where silver ants thrive.*	**a.** to focus on or emphasize the time, place, reason, or manner
b. *That was the day when Reeve's life changed forever.*	**b.** when the meaning of the head noun is specific
c./d. *The reason why he felt depressed was obvious.*	**c.** when the context is more formal: written as opposed to spoken English
	d. when the head noun is the subject of a sentence
Relative adverb + clause	Omit the head noun when:
a. *The ants know when to go back to their nests.*	**a.** the head noun has a general meaning (the time, the place)
b. *1939 is when World War II started.* (inferred: the year)	**b.** you can infer the head noun from the context
c. *Why he continues to live there is anybody's guess!* (not so formal)	**c.** the context of speech or writing is informal
Head noun + clause	Use this pattern:
a. *Can you please choose the hotel you wish to stay in as soon as possible?*	**a.** when the head noun has a specific meaning
b. *The reason you are not happy at work is not clear to us.*	**b.** when the context is formal

Test yourself

G. Read the sentences and decide whether or not the italicized words can be replaced by relative adverbs. Write those that can, using the relative adverb.

1. I like the restaurant *in which* we had a meal last week.
2. That's the restaurant *that* Kate is going to buy.
3. The day *on which* she had her first child was one of the happiest days of her life.
4. The months *in which* the flowers are prettiest are May and June.
5. The reason *that* he gave for not coming to work was derisory.
6. The reason *for which* I don't like winter is the dark, gloomy nights.
7. Running really fast over hot sand is *the way in which* you can avoid getting burned.
8. The year *that* was most difficult for me was 2002.
9. New students in a class have to get used to *the way in which* the teacher teaches.
10. I have no idea *which way* they went after they left Route 25.

Speaking focus

Leading a discussion

Encouraging participation: *Who would like to comment on that? Does anyone have anything to add?*

Bringing people in: *Dave, what do you think? Jan, do you want to add anything?*

Controlling a speaker: *Let's hear what other people have to say.*

Speeding up the discussion: *We only have five minutes left. We need to move along.*

Think about it

A. How is your life different from your parents' lives when they were your age? Make notes.

B. PAIR WORK Share your ideas with a partner. Which of these changes are positive? Which are negative?

C. GROUP WORK Together, choose ONE area of daily life that has changed in your country in the last 100 years (for example, food, clothes, houses). Work together to plan a short oral report, explaining the changes in people's lives and giving specific examples. All group members should take notes. Each group member should take a turn leading the discussion—your teacher will tell you when to switch. Use expressions from the box.

D. GROUP WORK Form a new group with students who prepared different reports. Take turns giving reports to your group. While you listen to the other students, take notes on the areas and the changes they discuss.

E. Talk about all the reports you heard and decide as a whole group: Which are the three most positive changes in life in your country? The three most negative changes?

In 1950, there were about 48 million cars in the world. By 1990, there were 310 million, and in 2002, there were almost 400 million.

FYI CO_2 = carbon dioxide

A. PAIR WORK Form expressions by matching the words on the left with the ones on the right.

EXAMPLE: *Many people are concerned about the destruction caused by acid rain.*

1. CO_2		**a.** layer
2. global		**b.** effect
3. acid		**c.** rain
4. the ozone		**d.** emissions
5. the greenhouse		**e.** warming

B. PAIR WORK Study the text to understand the words in bold. Then work with a partner and match the words with the definitions.

The Gwich'in, an **indigenous people** who live in the northern regions of Alaska, are not interested in becoming **fully paid-up** members of the **consumer society.** While they **embrace** certain aspects of modern living, such as telecommunications, they refuse to **compromise** their idyllic rural environment **in the interest of** progress. They fear that if they **make** too many **concessions** to oil **prospecting** or industrialization, their beautiful lakes, rivers, and streams will become polluted and their **verdant** mountains and valleys will turn into arid **wasteland.** Already, many of the animals they have hunted for years are in danger of extinction because their **natural habitats** are being destroyed by the effects of global warming. Like **conservationists** in other regions where natural resources and **cultural mores** are threatened by **so-called** progress, the Gwich'in want their children to **inherit** a world where they can **lead** simple, healthy lives, free from the problems they would encounter in industrialized areas.

1. customs of a society _____
2. receive as a gift from a relative or friend after the person's death _____
3. have or live _____
4. put at risk _____
5. places where animals live in the wild _____
6. looking for precious metals, minerals, etc._____
7. in order to help or support _____
8. people who have always belonged in a place _____
9. convinced or committed _____
10. way of life based on shopping and spending money _____
11. green and fertile _____
12. infertile area where vegetation no longer grows _____
13. accept enthusiastically _____
14. apparent _____
15. people who try or campaign to protect the environment _____
16. accept or agree to something unwillingly _____

C. With the class, list examples from your own society of the items in the box.

social mores	natural habitats	natural resources	conservation projects
indigenous people			

Listening strategy

Finding a time sequence

When reporting past events or telling a story, people sometimes don't tell the events in chronological order. Listening for words like *before, after,* and *when* can help you understand the sequence of events.

Before you listen

A. Have you ever spent time on a farm? What kinds of work do farmers do? What crops grow on farms near where you live or in other parts of the country?

First listening

B. You are going to listen to an elderly man named Albert talking about his memories of growing up on a farm in Indiana in the U.S. in the 1930s. Listen and write down the crops the family produced on their farm.

Second listening

C. Listen again. Write numbers from *1* to *7* to put the events in the correct chronological order. You will need to listen for *before, after,* and *when.*

_____ The family got their first car.

_____ A snake bit Albert's brother.

_____ The neighbors built a new barn.

_____ A flood covered the fields with water.

_____ Albert left the farm.

_____ Albert's mother died.

_____ There was a terrible fire.

After listening

D. Which things that Albert describes are similar to how rural life was in your country in the past? Are any parts similar to life in your country today? Would you like to live like this? Why or why not?

Test yourself

E. Listen to the talk and answer the question. Use time expressions to find the answer.

What was James Lee's first job?

a. teacher

b. government advisor

c. farmer

d. businessman

Writing an expository paragraph

Before you write

A. GROUP WORK First discuss what you see in the picture. Speculate about where it was taken and what the person is doing and say what you find surprising about the picture. Now, to find out more about the person in the picture, organize each of the groups of words into a sentence. Decide whether or not each sentence would make a good topic sentence.

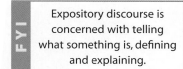

FYI Expository discourse is concerned with telling what something is, defining and explaining.

1. of / is / the / in / center / country / the / Evenkia / geographical / Russia / located
2. there / many / Evenkia / to / are / in / living / advantages
3. Evenks / hunting / reindeer / ride / the / when / go / they
4. many / serious / facing / Evenks / are / today / the / problems
5. are / Evenks / 3,000 / there / indigenous / approximately

B. In the same groups, read the sentences below and decide which is the topic sentence, which is the concluding sentence, and which are the supporting sentences. Then decide on the order of the supporting statements. Finally, copy the paragraph in the correct order.

1. The Evenks survive by hunting animals such as bears and squirrels.
2. Life for the Evenks, an indigenous people from central Russia, is becoming increasingly difficult.
3. When they go hunting, the Evenks do not ride horses.
4. Without their reindeer, the Evenks cannot go hunting.
5. Evenkia is a beautiful country with thick pine forests in the south fading to tundra in the north.
6. Unfortunately, the reindeer are becoming extremely scarce as the Evenks have exchanged a lot of reindeer meat for consumer goods, which oil prospectors bring to Evenkia.
7. The situation is so desperate that the governor of Evenkia has decided to buy five hundred reindeer from another region in the hope that this measure will save the Evenk people from extinction.
8. Because they cannot go hunting, the Evenks are running short of food and clothing and fuel.
9. Instead, they ride a unique subspecies of reindeer specially bred by them.

Write

C. Form new groups of four and think about an aspect of life in your country that is at risk of disappearing. It could be, for example, an animal, a language, an indigenous people, or simply a national custom. Then brainstorm and list all the things you know about this phenomenon. Write a coherent, mostly expository paragraph about it, making sure to choose your topic, supporting, and concluding sentences well.

A. GROUP WORK Work in groups of four and write a short quiz of ten questions about places, dates, reasons, and processes. Then form pairs with members of different groups and take turns asking each other the questions in your test. Remember to follow the pattern in the example answers. Keep score by giving one point for the correct information and one point for the correct pattern.

EXAMPLES:

1. *In which city did Elvis Presley die?*
   Memphis, Tennessee, is the city where Elvis died.

2. *Why do desert ants go out in the midday sun?*
   The reason why they go out at midday is to look for food.

B. PAIR WORK Think of a very special moment in your life that you recall. Think about the date, the place, and the reason why that memory is so special. Now share your memory with a partner and ask each other more detailed questions. Finally, tell the class what you learned about your partner.

C. CLASS TASK Organize a debate on this topic.

Progress through industrialization is the way for the world to go forward. Fears about the negative effects of global warming are totally exaggerated.

Men building Methanex gas plant, Chile.

Construction on Three Gorges Dam, China.

For more detail about Progress, view the CNN video. Activities to accompany the video begin on page 139.

Immigration

1 Warm Up

A. Describe these pictures. When and where do you think each picture was taken? Why do you think these people left their countries? What kinds of problems do you think they had when they got to their destination?

B. Work in pairs and practice the pronunciation of each of these countries. Then form the nationality adjective for each country.

Au**stra**lia	**Ca**nada	**E**gypt	**Ire**land	Ma**lay**sia	**Rus**sia
Af**ghan**istan	**Chi**le	France	**Is**rael	**Mex**ico	**Sau**di A**ra**bia
Argen**tin**a	**Chi**na	Greece	**It**aly	Pakis**tan**	Tai**wan**
Bosnia	Co**lom**bia	**In**dia	Ja**pan**	**Pe**ru	**Thai**land
Bra**zil**	**Con**go	Indo**nes**ia	Ko**rea**	**Por**tugal	**Tur**key
Cam**bo**dia	Do**min**ican Re**pub**lic	**I**ran	**Le**banon	Ro**man**ia	Viet**nam**

Communication
Describing migration patterns
Discussing the pros and cons of migration
Getting a turn in a conversation

Grammar
Stative and dynamic passives
Complex passives

Vocabulary
Review of countries and nationalities
Human emergencies and natural disasters

Skills
Skimming a text with statistics
Listening using written background information
Writing a paragraph with a preamble and topic sentence

FYI
Nationality adjectives can usually be made with one of these suffixes:
-ish, -(i/e)an, -ese, or *–i.*
Examples: *Spain: Spanish   Albania: Albanian   Argentina: Argentinean   Israel: Israeli*
Exceptions: *Dominican Republic: Dominican   France: French   Greece: Greek   Thailand: Thai   Peru: Peruvian   Afghanistan: Afghan*

C. Use the countries and adjectives for nationalities to talk about patterns of migration that you know about; for example, talk about migration patterns to or from your own country and about the effects they have had.

Reading strategy

Using statistical information

When a text has a lot of numbers and statistics, you can use charts, graphs, or visuals that help you clarify the general meaning of the text.

FYI net = the result after all the effects are known

Before you read

A. Study the map. Say which countries in the world had positive net migration between 1996 and 2001, which had negative net migration, and which had little or no net migration. Speculate about some possible reasons for these migration patterns.

NET MIGRATION AS PERCENT OF POPULATION AVERAGE, 1996-2001
NEGATIVE (-1% or more)   LITTLE OR NO NET MIGRATION (range of -0.99% to +0.99%)   POSITIVE (1% or more)

First reading

B. Skim the text and find the paragraphs that focus on these topics.

1. Origins of international immigrants _____
2. Effects of international immigration on some populations _____
3. Consequences of current U.S. policies on international immigration ____
4. Profile of the international immigrant ____
5. Current U.S. policies on immigration _____
6. Popular destinations of U.S. immigrants ____

Assembling the Future

How International Migrants Are Shaping the 21ST Century

By Rodger Doyle

1. The 150 million people who live outside the country of their birth make up less than 2.5% of the world population, but they have an importance far beyond their numbers. Some international migrants are
5 refugees or students, but those with the most **impact** are economic migrants drawn to places such as Los Angeles, where the **wages** may be three times greater than those in Mumbai (Bombay, India). These migrants tend to be young and willing to work for low wages. Though
10 traditionally **unskilled,** a growing number are highly educated.

2. Immigration is now the major contributor to **demographic** change in many developed countries. In the United States, according to the latest U.S. Census
15 Bureau projection,° the population will grow by 129 million in the period from 2000 to 2050, but if immigration stops, it would go up by just 54 million. Western Europe's population is 42% greater than that of the U.S., but its projected immigration is only about half
20 that of the U.S.; as a consequence, the region is expected to lose 28 million people over the next fifty years. Japan, which has close to zero net migration, is projected to lose 26 million by 2050. (Deaths will start overturning° births in Western Europe and
25 Japan around the middle of this decade.)

3. During the past six years, the U.S. received 27% of the world's international migrants, compared with 9% percent by Germany, the second most popular destination. (Western Europe as a whole, however, took
30 in 21%.) One fourth of all migrants to the U.S. went to California. Favorite cities, in order of the number of foreign-born, are Los Angeles, New York City, San Francisco, Miami, and Chicago.

4. International migrants primarily come from
35 developing countries, with China at 14% and Mexico at 8% being the largest sources. A few developing countries— Afghanistan, Bosnia,
40 Liberia, and Rwanda—have had significant influxes° in recent years, but these reflect mainly
45 the movement of refugees. Most developing countries had negative net migration.

5. In the past few years, every European country with considerable immigration has had a reaction against foreign workers, according to social scientist Christopher Jencks of Harvard University. Some Asian countries **hit hard** by recession° in the late 1990s tried to repatriate° migrant workers. Thus far the U.S. shows no signs of **reinstituting** the extremely restrictive° immigration laws of the past, a major reason being the dependence of many industries on a supply of foreign labor. Indeed, the AFL-CIO, once an opponent of high immigration quotas,° has **reversed** position and is now attempting to organize immigrants. This change in attitude, among other reasons, leads Jencks to conclude that a substantial reversal of the current **liberal** policies is unlikely.

6. That would be good news for employers and for the affluent° who can continue to buy goods and services on the cheap. The economy **as a whole** will benefit to the extent that cheap **labor** helps to control inflation.° But these immigration policies could be problematic. Can the U.S. economy really provide decent wages for the 46 million workers expected in the next fifty years? They may **depress** not only the wages of traditionally disadvantaged groups, such as blacks and Hispanics, but also the wages for American middle-class professionals, particularly if the U.S. continues to **relax** the rules for entry of high-tech workers.

Rodger Doyle can be reached at rdoyle2@adelphia.net. (*Scientific American* February 2002, page 20)

---

projection = prediction
overturning = becoming greater (in numbers) than
influx = sudden arrival of many people
recession = period of weak economic activity
repatriate = return people to their own country
restrictive = limiting or rigid
quota = fixed number
affluent = wealthy
inflation = rise in prices, alongside lowering in currency value

---

Second reading

C. Read the text again and find the reason or reasons for these statements.

1. International migrants have an importance far beyond their numbers. _____

2. Some countries such as Japan and Germany might have to reconsider their projected immigration programs. _____

3. International migrants come primarily from developing countries. _____

4. In the past few years, every European country with considerable immigration has had a reaction against foreign workers. _____

5. The U.S. does not intend to adopt the restrictive immigration policies of Western Europe. _____

6. The generous immigration policies of the U.S. government might have negative consequences for the country. _____

Vocabulary in context

D. Find a word or expression in **bold** in the text that has a similar meaning to an expression below.

1. relevant to population _____.
2. suffering from _____.
3. workers in general _____.
4. cause to be lower _____.
5. strong effect _____.
6. make weaker or less strict _____.
7. open-minded _____.
8. in general _____.
9. did the opposite _____.
10. bring back again _____.
11. payment by the hour for work _____.
12. not well trained, not professional _____.

Discussion

E. Discuss with the class what you understand by the expression, "The American Dream," and talk about its significance for the world in general, and for your country in particular.

Stative and dynamic passives

Complex passives

Practice

A. Complete the statements with the correct form (voice and tense) of the verb in parentheses. Then read the completed statements and decide where the agents in the box belong.

> by national governments   by the U.S. authorities
> by employers   by the U.S. Congress
> by the governments of their own countries

1. In the early 1990s, many illegal immigrants to the U.S. _____ (force) to return to their own countries.
2. In the late 1990s, however, immigration policies _____ (relax) and a lot of illegal immigrants _____ (give) permission to stay.
3. Owing to the rapid decline in the birth rate in some European countries, immigration laws _____ (currently review).
4. In most countries with immigrant populations, the jobs that _____ (offer) to the immigrants are those with the lowest wages.
5. Many immigrant workers will go back home if they _____ (guarantee) a decent standard of living.

B. Read the contrasting statements. The first is in the dynamic passive, and the second, in the stative passive. What in your opinion is the difference between the two?

1. **a.** Less restrictive immigration policies are being considered by many Western countries.
   b. The Great Wall of China is considered one of the wonders of the world.
2. **a.** Those new immigrant workers are being measured for their factory uniforms.
   b. Temperature is measured in degrees.
3. **a.** My home computer is being connected to the Internet today.
   b. My arm is connected to my shoulder.

4. **a.** Police say the illegal immigrants who are hiding in the jungle are being located with the aid of satellite technology.
   b. Mount Fuji is located in Japan.
5. **a.** My home is being used as an office these days.
   b. A thermometer is used to measure heat.

C. Complete the text with the correct passive forms of the verbs in parentheses.

Biologists in the south of France have found several forms of immigrant insects. The insects **(1)** _____ (classify) by a team of experts this month. The most common form of immigrant insect is the caterpillar of a moth, which **(2)** _____ (know) in scientific terms as *paysandisia archon*. The moth **(3)** _____ (regard) as a serious threat to the beautiful palm trees, which **(4)** _____ (find) all along France's Mediterranean coast, because the palms **(5)** _____ (slowly eat) by the moths. The increase in international trade and global warming means that France **(6)** _____ (colonize) by new insect species at an alarming rate.

D. PAIR WORK Decide which of the *passive constructions* are followed by a noun clause *(NC)* and which are followed by an infinitive clause *(IC)*.

1. *It is believed* that immigrant populations have an enriching effect on the host culture. __
2. *Western Europe is expected* to lose 28 million people over the next fifty years. __
3. *Japan is projected* to lose 26 million by 2050. __
4. *It was reported* recently that there is resistance in Western Europe to new immigrants. __
5. *Germany is said* to be the country in Western Europe that welcomes the highest number of immigrants. ___

E. Complete the sentences with passive constructions followed by a noun or an infinitive clause.

Although **(1)** ____(generally / assume)____ movements of populations between countries and across continents will continue to be a common feature of our modern world, **(2)** ____(also / believe)____ these movements will become increasingly difficult. Economic pressure is now affecting popular destinations for economic immigrants, so increasingly these immigrants **(3)** ____(think / be)____ the cause of higher rates of unemployment in the industrialized host countries. This is, however, simply not the case. In fact, **(4)** ____(frequently / report)____, because they work for low wages and do manual tasks, economic immigrants make an enormous contribution to a healthy economy. Thus, while the number **(5)** ____(expect / decline)____ in the next few decades, economic immigrants will continue to be regarded as a valuable commodity in industrialized societies.

Stative and dynamic passives	Explanations
Many verbs can be either stative or dynamic.	
1. She is being considered (by a special committee) for a job in the White House.	1. Dynamic passive verbs describe activities and can have or can omit the agent.
2. Gabriela Mistral is considered one of the greatest female poets in the world.	2. Stative passive verbs express states or conditions and do not have agents.
3. a. Mount Fuji is located in Japan. *3. b. Temperature is measured in degrees.* *3. c. Mexico is divided into states and a federal district.* *3. d. Radar is used to plot flight routes.* *3. e. My fingers are connected to my hands.* *3. f. Confucius is regarded as one of the greatest philosophers that ever lived.*	3. Stative passives are used to describe **(a)** location, **(b)** manner / method, **(c)** part-whole relationships, **(d)** purpose, **(e)** connection, and **(f)** reputation.

Complex passives	Explanations
1. It is reported that the number of illegal immigrants will increase as the world economic crisis deepens.	1. **Form:** Introductory *it* + passive verb + that (noun clause) **Use:** This form introduces a new topic with the new information at the end of the noun clause.
2. Today we are going to talk about the silver desert ant. The silver desert ant is believed to be one of the most resilient insects in the world.	2. **Form:** Subject (other than the introductory *it*) + passive verb + to + infinitive. **Use:** Can be used either to introduce a topic or just after the topic has been introduced.

Test yourself

F. Circle the correct construction in these statements.

1. In some countries, it *is commonly believed that / is commonly believing that* economic immigrants are prepared to do any kind of job for a very basic wage.
2. However, Pablo, who was an economic immigrant just a few years ago, *is currently being considered / is considered* for a job in the White House.
3. Work at the White House *is believing / is believed* to be very stressful.
4. Pablo, however, *is said / says* to be emotionally very resilient.
5. He *is briefing / is being briefed* by his new boss at the White House this week.
6. The White House, which *is being located / is located* in Washington, is the official residence of the president of the United States.

Speaking focus

Getting a turn in a conversation

Sometimes, in a group, other people are speaking so much that it's hard to get your turn. You can use these expressions to break into the conversation when there is a pause:

Could I just say something here?
Can I ask a question?
I have a point I want to make.
I have a question I'd like to ask.

A. PAIR WORK Why do people have to leave their homes and become refugees? What problems would you have if you suddenly had to move to another country tomorrow? Which countries now have a lot of refugees? Are there any refugees in your country?

B. GROUP WORK With your classmates, plan and carry out a mini-debate on this topic: *We should / should not allow refugees to enter our country.* Your teacher will assign you a position, which may or may not be your real opinion. With your team members, discuss ideas and fill in the chart. Use expressions from the box to take your turn in the discussion.

Position: We _____ allow refugees to enter our country.

Effect 1 _____ Explanation _____
Effect 2 _____ Explanation _____
Effect 3 _____ Explanation _____

C. GROUP WORK Now join with a team that discussed the opposite position. Tell them your reasons and explanations. Listen to the other team and take notes on their reasons. Then go back to your team. Talk about the other team's reasons, and think of arguments against them. Make notes. Then meet again with the other team and take turns giving your arguments against the other side.

D. What should be done to help refugees around the world?

According to the UN, there were 20 million refugees in the world in 2002, of whom 8.8 million lived in Asia, 4.8 million in Europe, and 4.1 million in Africa.

5 Vocabulary in Detail

A. Match these words or phrases with the definitions in 1–12.

a war	a flood
religious persecution	an earthquake
ethnic cleansing	a hurricane
economic hardship	a volcanic eruption
terrorism	a famine
racial discrimination	a drought

1. Killing by one group of people of all the people in another group that belong in the same cultural background
2. Use, often by minority groups, of violent methods, such as planting bombs and kidnapping, to reach political objectives
3. Long period without food caused by climatic extremes or war
4. Sudden, unexpected emission of smoke, fire, or lava from a high mountain
5. Fight with arms and bombs between two or more nations
6. Punishment of people whose faith is different from the official faith
7. Long period without rain, the result of which is that nothing grows
8. Having so little money that you cannot meet your basic needs
9. Sudden violent movement of the earth's surface
10. Putting a person at a great disadvantage because of his or her color
11. A large, violent rain and wind storm
12. Large quantities of water from rain or melting snows that cover land and houses that are not normally under water

B. In groups of four, use the words in exercise A to say why these dates and places are important.

EXAMPLE:
Kobe, Japan, in January 1995.
In January 1995, there was a terrible earthquake in Kobe, Japan.

1. The U.S. in the 1930s, Southeast Asia in the mid-1990s, Argentina in 2002
2. Vietnam from 1959 to 1975
3. The Sudan and Ethiopia very often
4. Bosnia in the early 1990s
5. Los Angeles, California in January 1994
6. The Caribbean and the east coast of the U.S., very frequently
7. Nevado del Ruiz, Colombia, in 1985
8. Yangtze River, China, in July 1995
9. Tokyo subway trains in March 1995
10. South Africa between 1948 and 1990
11. The Middle East and Northern Ireland for many years
12. Ireland in the 1840s and many countries in Africa today

C. GROUP WORK Brainstorm for all the words you know that are derived from the words in the box. Include their meanings and grammatical categories in your lists.

migrate persecute erupt destroy
contribute develop

Listening strategy

Using written background information

When you are answering a listening quiz or test, use the questions to provide you with useful background information. Carefully read the written information provided in the questions and charts before you listen.

Before you listen

A. You are going to listen to three teenaged immigrants to the United States. What kinds of problems might they have in adjusting to life in a new country?

B. Look at their names and their countries in the chart. What do you know about these countries?

First listening

C. Listen to them talk about their experiences and write their reasons for emigrating.

Name	Edward	Marta	Alexei
Country	China	Dominican Republic	Russia
Reason for emigrating			
Positive aspects of their new life			
Negative aspects of their new life			

Second listening

D. Listen again and take notes on the immigrants' experiences in the U.S.

After listening

E. In your opinion, which of these teenagers has been most successful in adjusting to life in a new country? Why?

Test yourself

F. Listen to Salma talking about her experiences coming to the U.S. from Pakistan. First, read the questions and consider what you know about Pakistan.

1. What caused the biggest problem for Salma?
   a. food **b.** language **c.** shopping **d.** clothes

2. How did she solve this problem?
   a. She studied English. **b.** She changed schools. **c.** She got a job. **d.** She made American friends.

7 Writing

Writing a paragraph with a preamble and topic sentence

Before you write

Preamble sentences often come right at the beginning of a paragraph. They give the reader a general idea of the subject of the paragraph or of a longer text (for example, an essay) but the reader is not able to tell from the preamble sentences what direction the text is going to take. Frequently, there is more than just one preamble sentence, especially at the beginning of a longer text.

A. GROUP WORK Read the information above about preamble sentences. Then decide which of the sentences in the pairs in 1–5 is a preamble sentence *(PS)* and which a topic sentence *(TS)*.

EXAMPLE:
> *Recently, immigration has been a topic of hot debate in Western Europe. (PS)*
> *In many Western European countries, economic immigrants have recently been the victims of different kinds of hostility. (TS)*

1. **a.** The recent flooding in Western Europe is no exception.
   b. Most natural disasters cause great distress to the populations they affect.

2. **a.** People interested in the customs and cultural mores of ancient civilizations often travel to the Middle East.
   b. A visit to the city of Palmyra, north of Damascus, is particularly inspiring.

3. **a.** Globalization has created greater opportunities for international cooperation and cultural exchanges.
   b. Biologists have discovered, however, that global trade has resulted in the arrival of unwelcome immigrant insects to some countries.

4. **a.** The senses of taste and smell are alike in some ways and different in others.
   b. Most normal human beings have both a sense of taste and a sense of smell.

5. **a.** It is common practice for animals to be used in scientific and medical experiments.
   b. Chimpanzees are often used because there are many ways in which they are similar to humans.

B. Organize these sentences into a coherent paragraph. Decide which sentence (or sentences) is the preamble sentence, which is the topic sentence, and which would make a good final sentence.

a. For example, the U.S. rose to greatness by employing and recycling workers who were rejected in Europe and by using forced labor from Africa.

b. Most societies all over the world have experience of migration in one form or another.

c. The British, on the other hand, benefited greatly from the skills and sweat of their fellow Europeans, specifically French Huguenots and Irish laborers.

d. What's more, it is undeniable that migrant-rich societies have amazing records of success.

e. In fact, it is hard to find an economic success story that has not had as its basis the work of immigrant populations.

f. Not to be forgotten in these success stories are countries like Peru and Brazil, which in the late 19th century made great economic progress, thanks to the hard work of immigrants from China and Japan.

Write

C. Write a four- to five-sentence paragraph on one of these topics. Try to introduce your paragraph with at least one preamble sentence.

a. The greatest natural threat to our country . . .

b. The most delicious ethnic food in our country . . .

c. The main cause of economic hardship in our country . . .

A. GROUP WORK Think of a person, a place, and a thing that are well known to other members of your class. Write out at least one sentence using the stative passive which helps identify the person, place, or thing.

EXAMPLES:
1. He is also known as The King. *Elvis Presley*
2. This country is divided into provinces. *Canada.*

Form pairs with a student from another group. Test one another with your statements. Now share your sentences and answers with the class.

B. Brainstorm with your teacher and list the names of the three most famous people and the three most famous places in your country. Brainstorm for all the things you are sure of about that person or place. Then work with a classmate and list all the things you think are true about the people or places but are not sure. Write stative passive statements using this information.

EXAMPLES:
Bill Gates is said to be a very generous philanthropist.
Tokyo is believed to be one of the most efficient cities in the world.

Then share your beliefs, thoughts, or rumors with the class.

C. CLASS TASK With the class, choose the topic from below that is relevant to your country's situation. Then hold a class debate.

1. Our immigrant populations have made our country a much better place.
2. The exodus of tens of thousands of people from our country on a regular basis has had a very negative effect on our culture and economy.

For more detail about Immigration, view the CNN video. Activities to accompany the video begin on page 140.

CO$_2$

1 Warm Up

A. PAIR WORK Match these words with the pictures. Then describe
the pictures and say what you know about the purpose of each
construction.

a fossil fuel plant   a windmill   a nuclear power plant   a solar collector

B. Place the phrases in the box under one of the headings.

Causes of pollution	Consequences of pollution	Solutions to pollution

> *recycling waste products such as bottles and cans*
> *emissions from the exhausts of vehicles*
> *global warming*
> *planting trees and other vegetation in our cities*
> *damage to the ozone layer*
> *pesticides used on crops*
> *using alternative sources of energy*
> *reforestation programs*
> *chemicals in rivers and oceans*
> *acid rain*
> *deforestation*
> *greenhouse effect*
> *garbage dumps*

C. Discuss which of the problems in B is the most serious in your
country and talk about how, if at all, the problem is being overcome.

Reading strategy

Looking out for markers of text organization

Although words such as *advantages / disadvantages* or *pros / cons* signal contrast, an experienced writer will often choose more sophisticated markers of text organization. Markers such as *the benefits / the difficulties, in support / in contrast* may be used, or the choice of positive or negative adjectives or verbs may indicate contrast.

Before you read

A. Describe what you see in this picture. Talk about the advantages and disadvantages of wind as a source of energy.

First reading

B. Skim the text and chose a suitable title from this list.

a. Finding Alternative and Renewable Sources of Energy

b. Solving the Problem of Waste Disposal

c. Sources of—and Solutions to—CO_2 Emissions

1. For the past thirty years, finding a solution to the greenhouse effect has been a major concern for research scientists. Although researchers do not always agree about the best ways to
5 repair and prevent future damage to the ozone layer, there does seem to be one consensus—namely, that solving the problem of high levels of carbon dioxide (CO_2) emissions is paramount, as this is the gas that is chiefly responsible for global warming. For some
10 scientists, the best solution to the problem is to exploit alternative sources of clean energy, such as wind power, solar power, and hydrogen. While progress has been made in the use of all of these, it is wind energy that, to date, represents the stiffest challenge to fossil fuels.
15 **2.** Wind power, the process by which the wind is used to **generate** mechanical power or electricity, has been **exploited** since early times to move ships, grind° grain, and pump° water. Records show that it was used to **propel** boats along the Nile River as early as 5000
20 B.C., and simple windmills for pumping water were in use in China several centuries before the beginning of the first **millennium.**
3. Wind power has many advantages. It is a free, infinite resource,° so supplies will not run out.° It is also
25 a source of clean, nonpolluting electricity. Unlike conventional° power **plants,** wind plants emit no air pollutants or greenhouse gases. In 1990, California's wind power plants prevented the emission of more than

2.5 billion pounds of
30 carbon dioxide, and 15 million pounds of other pollutants that would otherwise have been produced. It would take a forest of ninety to 175 million trees to provide the same air **quality.** Although the **initial** investment° in wind
35 power technology is higher than that for fossil fuel generators, 80% of that investment is for machinery,° with the remainder being spent on preparing and installing the site. Thus, in the long term, wind energy costs less as, once the plant is up and running, there is
40 no fuel to purchase and the **operating expenses** are minimal.
4. However, wind turbines are regarded by many people as **unsightly,** and the rotor blades of the turbines do produce some noise. Furthermore, birds
45 tend to get caught in the rotors and die as a result. For the most part, however, these problems are gradually being resolved or greatly reduced through technological developments and the **judicious** choice of sites° for the turbines, although the issue of **avian**
50 mortality still needs to be better understood. A major obstacle to using wind as a source of power is that it is **intermittent** and does not always blow when electricity is needed. By installing thousands of turbines throughout the country, this obstacle can also be

55 overcome, as there will always be enough turbines to harness the wind—no matter which way it blows!

5. Abandoning the use of fossil fuels, however, meets with great opposition in many countries, as it could cause major problems for the economy and lead to
60 the **sacrifice** of comfortable lifestyles. Thus, for some scientists, the solution to CO_2 emissions does not lie in the use of alternative sources of energy. Rather, these scientists **propose** that research should look for ways of absorbing the emissions that are more efficient than the
65 conventional planting of trees and other plants.

6. One Australian researcher has proposed that, if the **traditional** calcium carbonate-based Portland cement used in the construction industry were changed to a cement based on magnesium carbonate, almost every
70 construction in a city—from bridges to factories to apartment blocks—could **soak up** carbon dioxide. Emissions would also be drastically reduced at the production stage. Whereas a ton of CO_2 gases escapes into the atmosphere for every ton of Portland cement
75 produced, with the magnesium-based eco-cement,

emissions are almost halved. In addition, different types of refuse, such as plastics, rubbers, and agricultural waste, can be used as a bulking° material in the mixing of this cement, thus contributing to the easing of
80 another environmental problem—that of waste disposal. The main difficulty with eco-cement is that the building industry is very conservative, but as the need to solve the problem of CO_2 emissions becomes increasingly urgent, eco-cement may still have its day.

---

grind = reduce to very small pieces
pump = raise
resource = commodity
run out = finish
conventional = usual, customary
investment = money spent to establish a business
machinery = all the machines in one place
site = specific place for a construction
bulking = making thicker

Second reading

C. Work in groups and write your own outline notes for the text. Use these questions as a guide.

1. What problem is discussed?

2. What are the two main solutions proposed?

3. What are the advantages and disadvantages of solution 1? Give examples.

4. What are the advantages and disadvantages of solution 2? Give examples.

Vocabulary in context

D. Find the following words and expressions in the text and match them with the phrases on the right. The paragraph number and line number are given for each word.

1. repair (1.5)
2. consensus (1.6)
3. paramount (1.8)
4. to date (1.13)
5. be up and running (3.39)
6. on the debit side (4.42)
7. easing (6.79)
8. have its day (6.84)

a. function well
b. up to this point in time
c. enjoy success
d. a disadvantage is that
e. very important, crucial
f. reduction
g. complete agreement
h. fix

E. Which **bolded** words or expressions in the text have the same or similar meanings to the words below?

Paragraph 2
period of 1,000 years
produce
used for a specific purpose
move forward with force

Paragraph 3
beginning
land and buildings used for an industry
standard
cost of running a business

Paragraph 4
irregular
ugly or unattractive
wise
relevant to birds

Paragraphs 5 and 6
absorb
the loss
suggest
conventional

Discussion

F. With the whole class, discuss specific places in your country where CO_2 emissions are a problem. Discuss the sources of the emissions. Which of the approaches in the reading would you use to try to solve the problems if you were a member of your government? Give reasons for your choice and discuss any other suggestions you have for solving the problem.

More passive forms
The role of passive in cohesion

A. Match these grammatical descriptions with the *passive structures* in the sentences.

present perfect	modal + *have been* +
modal + *be* + past	past participle
participle	past perfect progressive
past progressive	present simple
past perfect	past conditional
future *(will)*	past simple

1. In order to find renewable sources of energy, new technologies *will be developed.*
2. The problem of global warming *might not be solved* in the next fifty years.
3. The wind *is used* to generate mechanical power.
4. The wind *has been exploited* since early times to move ships.
5. Windmills *were used* in China for several centuries before the first millennium.
6. A huge amount of carbon dioxide *would have been produced.*
7. We saw that many young trees *were being planted* to reduce the effects of deforestation.
8. Deforestation occurred because thousands of trees *had been cut down* for the logging industry.
9. For many years, some environmental scientists *had been warning* governments about the negative consequences of deforestation.
10. The problem of global warming *should have been solved* years ago.

B. Complete the text with passive constructions using the correct tenses and forms of the verbs in parentheses.

Since early times, advances in science and technology **(1)** _____ *(consider)* important for humankind. Without them, cures for serious diseases **(2)** _____ *(not / find)* and improve-ments in industrialization processes **(3)** _____ *(reduce)*. Often, however, concern **(4)** _____ *(express)* at the damage scientific progress causes to the environment. Even today, efforts **(5)** _____ *(still / make)* to solve the problems that resulted from the unchecked industrialization of Western countries in the19th and 20th centuries, when rivers **(6)** _____ *(pollute)* as a result of toxins from factory waste and unhealthy living conditions **(7)** _____ *(create)* in big cities because of emissions and waste. Nowadays, in most countries, the consequences for the environment of advances in science **(8)** _____ *(must / study)* before new inventions **(9)** _____ *(accept)* by governments; but already a lot of damage **(10)** _____ *(do)* to our planet.

Interact

C. PAIR WORK In pairs, discuss the topics below.

- What is being done to prevent or cure diseases that are common in your country?
- What improvements in communication systems have been made in the last fifty years in your country?
- What do you think will be invented in science and technology in the next ten years?

D. Look at the two examples below and discuss why you think the second sentence or second part of the sentence has a passive construction. Use the information in parentheses after each of these first sentences to write two cohesive sentences (Example 1) or one single sentence with a relative clause (Example 2).

EXAMPLES:
1. *In July 2002, a team of Colombian scientists discovered a flock of fourteen indigo-winged parrots. These parrots were first seen in the wild in 1911.*
2. *The indigo-winged parrot lives near the summit of Colombia's highest volcano, which is often covered in fog.*

1. Environmentalists would like to abandon fossil fuels in favor of wind power. (People have used wind power since ancient times.)

2. Scientists are exploring ways of reducing CO_2 emissions. (The combustion engine produces CO_2 emissions.)

3. In some regions of the world, governments are considering the possibility of reducing emissions by using eco-cement. (A researcher in Australia has invented eco-cement.)

4. Global warming has increased over the past fifty years because of the hole in the ozone layer. (Greenhouse gases have caused the hole in the ozone layer.)

More passive forms	Explanation and examples
Passives with verb tenses	Use *be* + past participle and the corresponding tense of the verb.
a. past progressive	a. *We were being followed.*
b. present perfect	b. *The forests have been destroyed.*
c. past perfect	c. *The birds had first been seen in the wild in 1911.*
d. future *(will)*	d. *The birds will be protected from now on.*
e. conditional	e. *More emissions would have been produced if we had not switched to wind energy.*
Passives with modal verbs	Use the corresponding tense of the modal verb + *be* + past participle.
a. modal + *be* + past participle	a. *Eco-cement should be substituted for normal cement.*
b. modal + *have been* + past participle	b. *The problem should have been solved years ago.*
Passives to create cohesion	
a. In English, the subject of a sentence contains the focus. Often a new topic is introduced at the end of a sentence and this then becomes the focus or subject of the next sentence. To make a smooth transition to the new focus or subject, the passive voice is often used. This creates cohesion and makes it easier for the reader to understand the change of focus.	a. *Researchers have recently found the remains of the ancient city under the sea near Alexandria in Egypt. The city has been positively identified as Heracleion.*
b. Often a synonym for the topic in the first sentence is used in the second sentence together with passive voice to create cohesion.	b. *Scientists have recently spotted the indigo-winged parrot in Colombia's highest volcano. This beautiful bird was last seen in the wild in 1911.*

Test yourself

E. Complete the paragraph with the correct form and tense of the active or passive voice of the verbs in parentheses.

In July 2002, a team of Colombian scientists discovered a flock of fourteen indigo-winged parrots. These birds were first seen in the wild in 1911 but **(1)** _____ *(believe)* to have become extinct. The indigo-winged parrot **(2)** _____ *(consider)* to be the most brightly colored of all birds. The sighting of the fourteen birds in July 2002 **(3)** _____ *(occur)* at a height of ten thousand feet, near the summit of Colombia's highest volcano. The volcano **(4)** _____ *(say)* to be the only place where these fabulous birds **(5)** _____ *(live)*. The leader of the scientists who **(6)** _____ *(spot)* the birds said: "A parrot's sharp cry **(7)** _____ *(pierce)* the gloom and **(8)** _____ *(follow)* by a chorus of others. It **(9)** _____ *(be)* like watching a miracle from heaven as one of the world's rarest birds **(10)** _____ *(descend)* before our eyes."

Checking a listener's understanding

When you are speaking about a complicated subject, it's a good idea to check and see if your listeners understand you. Some expressions you can use:

Informal ——————→ Formal

Got that? Okay so far? Do you see what I mean? Do you follow me? Is that clear?

A. PAIR WORK What did you throw away yesterday? Tell your partner about everything you can remember. How many bags of garbage does your family usually throw away in a week? Do you know what happens to your garbage after you throw it away?

B. GROUP WORK Situation: You are members of an organization called People for a Better World. Your country is facing a serious environmental problem—too much garbage and no place to put it. Together with your group, design and make a poster giving suggestions about ways people can produce less garbage. First, make a list of ideas. Use expressions from the box to check your group members' understanding. Decide on the best ideas. Then work together to express your ideas in words and pictures in your poster.

C. Hang your poster on the classroom wall. Take turns with your group members: have one person stand next to the poster to explain the ideas, while the others walk around the room looking at other groups' posters. Then switch roles.

D. What new ideas did you get from the posters? Which of these things would be easy to do?

The British throw away 2.5 billion disposable diapers every year. The Japanese throw away 30 million disposable cameras every year.
The average Mexican throws away almost 300 kilos of garbage per year, the average Norwegian about 640 kilos, and the average American over 700 kilos.

5 Vocabulary in Detail

A. Match the one-word verbs on the right with the *phrasal verbs* in these sentences.

1. When they are burned, fossil fuels *give off* carbon dioxide and other greenhouse gases.
2. Greenhouse gases *soak up* heat that should escape into the atmosphere.
3. Temperatures on earth *go up* when fossil fuels are burned.
4. Animals in the upper levels of a rain forest *feed on* plants and insects.
5. In most rain forests, too many trees are *cut down* and used for wood.
6. Global warming is so serious that fertile lands *are turning into* desert in some regions of the world.
7. When animals lose their natural habitats, they *die out.*
8. Soon all our natural resources will be *used up* if we do not reduce our levels of consumption.

  a. become
  b. disappear
  c. produce
  d. finish
  e. fell
  f. absorb
  g. eat
  h. rise

B. Match the phrasal verbs in the dialog with the *one-word* verbs in the list.

S1: I think we should (1) *cut down on* the amount of paper we use in this office.

S2: I'd (2) *go along with* that and I am glad you (3) *brought* the topic *up,* as I'd like to (4) *go through* a few more environmental friendly measures we could take.

S1: Great, I'd like to hear about those, but do you think we could (5) *put* the discussion *off* until this afternoon. I have to go to a meeting at the bank.

S2: Sure, what time do you (6) *get back*?

S1: About 2 p.m., if we (7) *get down to* business early.

S2: Okay, see you when you get back and we can (8) *talk over* the environmental issues.

  a. start
  b. postpone
  c. support
  d. reduce
  e. discuss
  f. return
  g. list
  h. suggest

C. Study the classification of the verbs from exercises A and B and use them in contexts of your own choosing.

Phrasal verb summary

Must never separate	Must separate with both noun and pronoun objects	Must separate with pronoun objects; can separate with nouns
go up	turn into	give off
feed on	Note: *Turn into* can also be classified in column 1.	cut down
die out		soak up
cut down on	*She turned into a beautiful woman even though she was rather unattractive as a child.*	use up
go along with		bring up
go through		put off
get back		talk over
get down to		

Before you listen

A. You are going to listen to a talk on how your food affects the environment. What do you think it will include?

First listening

B. Listen to the talk and write down the three main ideas.

1. _____ 2. _____ 3. _____

Second listening

C. Listen again and take notes on the supporting details.

After listening

D. PAIR WORK Look at your notes and work together to write three questions about the ideas in the talk.

E. PAIR WORK Work with a new partner. Take turns asking and answering the questions.

Test yourself

F. Listen to the talk and answer the question.
What is the speaker's main idea?

a. Pollution has gotten much worse in the last twenty years.

b. This city needs to have more buses.

c. Air pollution can cause illness in children.

d. Public transportation is too expensive.

7 Writing

Writing a paragraph with preamble, topic, support, and conclusion

Before you write

A. Work in groups of four and discuss what you know about these places and topics.

> Los Angeles   Mexico City   Sao Paulo   Singapore   smog
> high import tax on cars   electric cars
> a day a week when cars cannot be driven
> very good and cheap public transport   alcohol-fueled cars

B. In the same groups, organize these sentences into a coherent paragraph. Remember to distinguish between the preamble sentence/s, the topic sentence, the supporting sentences, and the concluding sentence.

1. The electric car draws its power from a battery.
2. All over the world, governments are trying to reduce emissions from motor vehicles.
3. California hopes to convert soon to using mostly electric vehicles. So, if the experiment works, many other cities and countries all over the world might follow its example.
4. But is the electric car really emission-free?
5. Another major disadvantage of the electric car is that the batteries are heavy and the car tends to be rather slow, especially when the battery is getting low.
6. Thus, it has the advantage that, in the first instance, it does not produce emissions.
7. For many, the electric car is the solution to an emission-free environment.
8. What's more, it tends not to be very big and is ideal for short journeys.
9. A potential problem with the electric car is that it could still generate emissions if the plants that produce the electricity for the batteries use fossil fuels.

Write

C. Write a paragraph on one of these topics. Don't forget to include at least one preamble sentence.

> My Favorite Car   Little Ways to Help the Environment
> The Ideal City to Live In   My Favorite Landscape

D. PAIR WORK Find a partner who has written a paragraph on a different topic and read each other's work. Comment on the organization of each other's paragraphs and make suggestions to improve them. Read your paragraph aloud to the class.

A. GROUP WORK Work in groups of four and, with reference to all the phrasal verbs you know, write a phrasal verb quiz. The quiz should consist of explainations of the meaning of the phrasal verbs without using them. After designing your quiz, get together with another group and test the group with your quiz.

EXAMPLE: *This is what you do when you get too tired or too frustrated to continue with something.*   **Give up**

B. GROUP WORK Work in groups of four and list all the positive and negative aspects about the city you live in or the nearest big city to you. Then write notes about all the things you think should be done to solve the problems. Imagine you are city planners, and use your notes to prepare an oral presentation of your new plans for the city. Practice giving the oral presentation in your groups. Then choose a representative for your group. Give your oral presentation and listen to those of the other groups. Then discuss the ideas you have all proposed. Say which you think are practical, or too expensive, or not feasible, and why.

C. CLASS TASK Discuss the topic as a class.

The private car is the cause of some of the world's greatest problems.

For more detail about CO_2, view the CNN video. Activities to accompany the video begin on page 141.

Review Unit 2

Review Your Grammar

A. Rewrite each sentence using the passive form. Keep the same meaning.

1. Someone found Barbara's stolen car. _____
   _____

2. Laws protect some natural resources. _____
   _____

3. They saw some graylings in the shallow water. _____
   _____

4. Volunteers returned the animals to their natural habitat. _____
   _____

5. Someone provides food for the pigeons in the park on a daily basis. _____
   _____

6. They use information from the Internet to update their files. _____
   _____

B. Rewrite the answers you wrote in exercise A, changing all present and past tense passives to future passives.

EXAMPLE:
1. _Barbara's stolen car will be found._

2. _____
   _____

3. _____
   _____

4. _____
   _____

5. _____
   _____

6. _____
   _____

High Challenge

C. Circle the letter of the underlined word or phrase in each sentence that is incorrect.

1. I <u>can't</u> remember the name of the movie theater <u>that</u> we <u>saw</u> <u>that</u> movie last week.
     A   B   C   D

2. He <u>had chosen</u> <u>to take</u> the 5:00 train, <u>which</u> is often very <u>crowd</u>.
       A   B   C   D

3. Paris <u>regards</u> as one of the <u>most</u> beautiful cities <u>that</u> the world has ever <u>known</u>.
         A   B   C   D

4. Gary <u>was seen</u> to leave early, <u>that</u> <u>caused</u> his friends <u>to ask</u> questions.
          A   B   C   D

5. The weather <u>is expect</u> to get warmer <u>during</u> <u>the</u> next century, which <u>will cause</u> problems.
              A   B   C   D

Review Your Vocabulary

A. Circle the word that doesn't belong.

1. high   affluent   deep   flat
2. grayling   caribou   mouse   crop
3. crow   vegetation   forest   grass
4. river   ocean   canyon   stream
5. mountain   drought   hurricane   flood
6. recession   inflation   millennium   wages

B. Match each sentence with its communication goal within a discussion.

___ 1. Lisa, what do you have to say?
___ 2. We have only a few minutes left.
___ 3. Does anyone want to add anything?
___ 4. Let's hear what someone else has to say.
___ 5. Are there any other ideas we haven't considered?
___ 6. Who wants to comment on that?
___ 7. So Bill, do you want to add anything?
___ 8. We need to move along now.

a. encouraging participation
b. bringing specific people in
c. controlling a speaker
d. speeding up the discussion

C. Check (✓) the best response.

1. Does the U.S. have many natural resources?
   ___ Yes, but it is running out of natural gas.
   ___ Yes, but it is putting off the use of cloning.
2. What kind of economic hardship have some countries endured?
   ___ Some countries have experienced ethnic cleansing.
   ___ Inflation has been a big problem in some places.
3. Is the U.S. economy always strong?
   ___ No, there are intermittent recessions.
   ___ No, it is sometimes bitter.
4. I see your company has invested in some new machinery.
   ___ Yes, they're cutting down on new machines.
   ___ Yes, and it's already up and running.
5. What do you think about consumer societies?
   ___ They're great! I'm a fully paid-up member of one.
   ___ They're terrible! I can't stand religious persecution.
6. What happened to all the fish in Lake Montego?
   ___ They wore out.
   ___ They died out.

FYI Some words have positive associations and others, negative. For example, the word *too* has a negative association, so if you say that a country is *too powerful,* this implies a criticism. As you learn new words, find out if they have positive or negative associations, so that you can use them correctly.

Review Your Speaking

Fluency

Rio de Janeiro, Brazil

Arch de Triomphe, Paris, France.

A. PAIR WORK Look at the pictures and discuss the questions below with your partner.

- Which city would you like to live in for a short period? Why?
- What famous places can you name in each city?
- What famous people live in or come from each city?
- What is one product that each city is famous for?
- If you have visited one of these cities, suggest one way the environment there could be improved.

F•A•Q

I am going to have an oral test. How can I prepare?

First of all, you need to think about whether the test is going to be just you who is talking to the examiner, or you with another candidate and the examiner or examiners. If the test is one-to-one, then the examiner will ask you questions and want you to speak as much as you can on the topic. It's useful to think ahead about the type of questions that are usually asked and be ready to answer. It is common to be asked questions about yourself (hobbies, likes, dislikes, etc.), your family, your city, or your country. Thinking ahead about how you could answer such questions will make you feel more confident.

If there is another candidate with you in the examination, then you must take turns speaking. Don't try to dominate the conversation. Encourage the other person to speak. Don't interrupt.

Review Your Listening

A. Thinking about what you already know about a subject can help you to understand what you hear. You are going to listen to four people talking about getting a new car.

- What are some reasons why people get a new car?
- What things do they consider in choosing a car?
- How do cars affect the environment?
- Which kinds of cars have the biggest impact on the environment?

Listening 1

B. Listen to the conversation. Why does Ginny want to get a new car?

C. Listen again. Write numbers to put the events in order.

_____Ginny got in an accident.

_____Ginny joined Save the Earth.

_____Ginny's husband bought an SUV.

_____Ginny bought a very small car.

_____Ginny got married.

Listening 2

D. Listen to the second part of the conversation. Do the other three people agree with Ginny?

E. What do these people think Ginny should do? Write down their opinions.

Dave thinks Ginny should _____ because _____

_____.

Frank thinks Ginny should _____ because _____

_____.

Sue thinks Ginny should _____ because _____

_____.

Innovations

1 Warm Up

A. Describe what you see in the pictures. Discuss approximately when each invention first appeared, what purpose(s) it fulfills, and the ways in which it changed the world.

B. PAIR WORK In pairs, use one of the words in the box to complete the sentences.

1. That store sells computer _____ such as printers, computers, and scanners.
2. A _____ is a tiny piece of silicon that bears many integrated circuits.
3. A _____ is a printed version of computerized material.
4. You _____ something _____ if you want to read it in hard copy form.
5. A _____ is a machine that works like a computer because it is connected to one.
6. A _____ is a system of communication between different computers or terminals.
7. A _____ is a computer program that manages the shared access to a network.
8. _____ is another way of saying to keep information in a computer.
9. A _____ is the screen where computer information appears.
10. The programs for computers that help us perform operations are the _____.
11. We _____ files from a network or server and store them in our own computers.
12. When a network is not working properly, it _____.
13. _____ is another way of saying finding information using a computer.
14. _____ means we have access to the Internet.

C. GROUP WORK Write a list of the four most important inventions in the past 100 years and discuss their benefits and any problems they have caused.

Communication
Discussing the Web and other innovations
Debating medical research and patents
Offering suggestions

Grammar
Reduced adverb clauses

Vocabulary
Computer-related terms
Phrasal verbs used in research
Science collocations

Skills
Interpreting a scientific journal article
Listening to instructions
Writing introductory paragraphs

---

software terminal server hard copy store data access data microchip monitor download is down network print out hardware be online

Before you read

A. In groups, discuss what you think the idiomatic expressions in the box might mean. Then match each one with the **bolded** words in the statements.

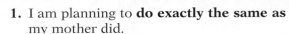

> pursue a dream   turn one's back on   not look back
> follow in the footsteps of   be nothing short of

1. I am planning to **do exactly the same as** my mother did.
2. After his initial success, he **never stopped and went on** to become a great scientist.
3. Although he was poor as a child, he **rejected the opportunity** to make a lot of money when he became an adult.
4. My dinner party **was a complete** failure. I burned almost everything.
5. Very often, we achieve great things if we **follow our purest ambitions.**

First reading

B. Scan the text and decide if the following statements are True (T) or False (F). Correct the false statements and identify the information in the text that supports the true ones.

1. By 1991, a lot of people in the world had access to the World Wide Web (WWW). _____
2. Tim Berners-Lee followed in his parents' footsteps. _____
3. Tim was able to buy a 6800 microchip in the mid-1970s because microchips were no longer so expensive. _____
4. Tim strongly believed that only certain people should have access to the Web. _____
5. People all over the world are grateful to DNA research companies. _____
6. DNA research companies are greatly concerned for the patient's welfare. _____
7. Pharmaceutical companies might start to do what the research companies have been doing. _____
8. Monopolies on gene patents and on the drugs which act on the genes are a natural and logical development in medical research. _____

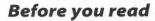

Reading strategy

Using your knowledge of word families

When you come across an unfamiliar word in a text, try to think of a word you know that this new word might be related to. To test your hypothesis, take into account the context in which the unfamiliar word appears. For example, the word *proposal* (noun) might make you think of the word *propose* (verb), the word *payment* (noun) will suggest *pay* (verb), and so on.

Patents and Profits

1. It is hard to believe that in 1991, what is now commonly known as "the Web" consisted of just twelve computer servers worldwide and **barely** five hundred in 1993. It is perhaps equally hard to believe that by the
5 end of 1994, it consisted of ten thousand. Now affecting the lives of millions of people, the Web has **revolutionized** our world. That so many people have access to the most **radical** advance in information technology since the invention of the printing press° in

10 the middle of the 15th century is largely due to the philanthropic° attitude of one of its most enthusiastic and **persevering pioneers.**
    2. Born in London in 1955, Tim Berners-Lee is a product of the computer age. His parents worked on
15 the Ferranti 1, the world's first commercial computer, and as a child, he spent hours with his father discussing ways of **linking** computers and enabling them to make connections between apparently unconnected facts. When cheap microchips became available in the mid-
20 1970s, Berners-Lee bought a 6800 microchip and by

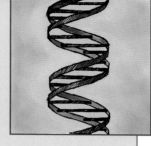
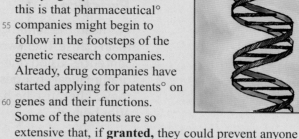

the spring of 1976, had wired it up to a homemade monitor and produced his first PC. This achievement gave him the **impetus** to pursue his childhood dream of exploiting to the fullest the latent° power of computers.
25 After designing software for his own and his company's **purposes,** Berners-Lee produced, in 1989, a radical **proposal** for storing, accessing, and updating information via computer networks. From then onwards and with the help of hypertext, invented by the American
30 Ted Nelson thirty years earlier, he never looked back, going on to **set up** the first computer "server" in 1990. However, in contrast to other Internet whiz kids, Berners-Lee firmly turned his back on the opportunity to become a billionaire. Instead, when his bosses talked of
35 charging for Web access, he insisted° that it would limit its growth and create a World Wide Web elite.

3. Just as great advances have been made in Internet communication over the past few decades, similar **strides** have been made in medical science. Genetic
40 research has developed DNA tests that assess, for example, a person's risk of developing certain types of cancer. One would expect companies dedicated to this kind of research to be extremely popular, but this is not the case. Unlike Berners-Lee, some pioneers in genetic
45 testing have gotten **greedy.** They are insisting that the genes they have discovered are their private **property** and are trying to stop other institutions from using the tests unless they pay. Critics° of the research companies claim that they **are looking to** profit at patients' expense
50 and that the resulting monopolies° created by such payment policies would allow the companies to charge unreasonable prices for their tests.

4. Perhaps the most worrying implication° of all this is that pharmaceutical°
55 companies might begin to follow in the footsteps of the genetic research companies. Already, drug companies have started applying for patents° on
60 genes and their functions. Some of the patents are so extensive that, if **granted,** they could prevent anyone else from touching those genes to create drugs that act on them, or even from testing the genes for mutations°
65 in a patient. Arguments that monopolies will not thrive seem to forget the potentially huge rewards on offer to a company that controls the diagnosis and treatment of a common **disease.** As more patents become available, pharmaceutical companies may find it hard to resist the
70 large amounts of money they can make by monopolizing them. This, many people argue, would be nothing short of disastrous for society.

---

printing press = large machine for printing the written word
philanthropic = unselfish, looking to help other people or society in general
latent = present, but not yet developed
insist = say emphatically
critics = people who complain about or find fault with something
monopoly = control of an entire market by one person or company
implication = suggestion, theoretical outcome
pharmaceutical = related to medicines
patent = exclusive, legal right to an invention or process
mutations = genetic changes

Second reading

C. Answer the questions by reading and interpreting the meaning of the text.

1. Why did Tim Berners-Lee pursue his dream of establishing computer networks?

2. Why did he turn his back on becoming a billionaire?

3. What made it possible for Berners-Lee never to look back with respect to his research?

4. Why is it worrying that big pharmaceutical companies might follow in the footsteps of genetic research companies?

Vocabulary in context

D. Find a word or expression in **bold** in the text that has the same or a similar meaning to each of the following meanings.

1. **Paragraph 1:** extreme, the leader in a new area of knowledge, changed completely, hardly, determined

2. **Paragraph 2:** energy, objective or intention, get ready or organize, suggested plan, connecting

3. **Paragraph 3:** wanting more than is necessary, advances, exclusive right, try or plan to

4. **Paragraph 4:** illness, allowed or permited

Discussion

E. Discuss which of the two innovations described in the text has contributed most to humankind. Give your reasons.

Reduced adverb clauses

Practice

A. Read the sentences that each contain a **reduced adverb clause** and a main clause. Then, working in groups, write out complete versions of the sentences, using one of these words or expressions and making the necessary grammatical changes: while they were ... which were ...
they ... because he had never ... because we ... as they were ...
after he had ...

EXAMPLE:

Having designed software for his own purposes, Berners-Lee produced a radical proposal for exploiting computer networks.
After he had designed software for his own purposes, Berners-Lee produced a radical proposal for exploiting computer networks.

1. **Taking the bus into work every day,** we help to limit CO2 emissions.
2. **Fascinated by the indigo-winged parrot,** the researchers spent days looking for them on Colombia's highest volcano.
3. **Waiting near the summit of the volcano,** the scientists spotted the birds.
4. The scientists started to take pictures, **trying hard not to make too much noise.**
5. The birds, **frightened by the presence of the scientists,** disappeared really quickly again.
6. **Not having ever been seriously ill before,** Reeve suffered a deep depression after his accident.

B. Reduce the full adverb clauses in these sentences.

EXAMPLE:

Because Pete was feeling depressed, he decided to take a vacation.
Feeling depressed, Pete decided to take a vacation.

1. Since he and his wife had never had a lot of money, they had not traveled much before.
2. Because they had some friends in Mexico, they decided to go there.
3. While they were packing for their trip, they heard of the earthquake.
4. As they were shocked by the news, they decided to postpone their trip.
5. After they postponed their trip a few months, they eventually went and had a fabulous time.

C. GROUP WORK Complete these statements about yourself. Share the information about yourself with a partner. Tell the class what you learn about your partner, using either the reduced or full form of the adverb clause.

1. (Not) having studied hard at high school, I _____.
2. Before coming to class today, I _____.
3. Exhausted after my busy week, last weekend I _____.
4. After having had a wonderful weekend, on Monday I _____.
5. Having relaxed on the weekend, I _____.

D. Work alone and match the main clauses on the right with the **reduced adverb clauses** on the left. Compare your answers with a partner's.

1. Situated high in the Andes Mountains,
2. Grown in temperate zones,
3. Producing lots of emissions,
4. Not having learned Spanish,
5. Being a clean and infinite source,
6. Maintaining their respect for nature,
7. Having lived for a long time in Japan,
8. Often ignored by international travelers,

a. she became a great sushi fan.
b. industry has polluted our air.
c. Pakistan is a fascinating country.
d. the Arctic Villagers will survive.
e. Bolivia is a fantastic country.
f. wind energy is harmless.
g. coffee is a popular cash crop.
h. he found life in Mexico difficult at first.

Reduced adverb clauses

Rules	Examples
The adverb clause can only be reduced if the subject in both the main clause and the adverb clause is the same.	**Correct:** *Living in Peru,* I learned a lot of Spanish. **Incorrect:** *Living in Peru,* Peruvian friends took me to the beach every summer. **Correct:** When I was living in Peru, Peruvian friends took me to the beach every summer.
Reduced adverb clauses can come at the beginning, in the middle, or at the end of a sentence. Commas are needed in all positions.	*Being a keen bird watcher,* Paul is fascinated by the news of the indigo-winged parrot. Paul, *being a keen bird watcher,* is fascinated by the news of the indigo-winged parrot. Paul is fascinated by every detail, *reading all the research articles on the topic he can find.*
When the **adverb** is included, commas are not required.	Paul saw some of the birds in Colombia *while living **there*** in 2002.

Test Yourself

E. Decide which of these statements are grammatically correct. Correct the incorrect ones.

1. Having packed their luggage, Gavin and Paula went to bed early.
2. It was a bright sunny morning, getting up at 6 a.m.
3. Excited at the thought of their trip, they could barely eat breakfast.
4. Calling for a taxi, the driver arrived at 7 a.m. sharp.
5. It began to rain, arriving at the airport.
6. Delighted at the prospect of getting away from such awful weather, they began to feel really excited.
7. After sleeping for much of their twelve-hour flight, their airplane landed in Seoul.
8. Mexico, bounded by the U.S. and Guatemala, proved to be one of the most fascinating countries they had ever visited.

Speaking focus

Offering suggestions

To make a suggestion, we can say: *What about ...? How about ...? We could .... Why don't we ...? Maybe we should ...*

To accept a suggestion: *That's a great idea. Why don't we try that? That sounds like a good idea.*

To reject a suggestion politely: *I'm not sure that's a good idea. I'm not sure that will work. I don't know about that.*

A. PAIR WORK What things do you use in your daily life that people didn't have ten years ago? Have these things changed your life?

B. GROUP WORK Imagine you are members of a research team at a small company and you have developed a wonderful new invention. You are going to have a meeting to decide what to do with your invention. Prepare and practice a role play to present to the class. Write short notes to help you remember important points. Try to use some of the expressions for making and rejecting suggestions in your role play. Then take turns presenting your role plays to the class.

> **Role 1:**
> You are the president of the company. You want your company to make as much money as possible.

> **Role 2:**
> You are a scientist. You want this invention to make you and your company famous.

> **Role 3:**
> You are a scientist. You want to produce this invention very cheaply to help people around the world.

> **Role 4:**
> You are from the marketing department. You have an idea to sell lots of this invention.

C. CLASS TASK Discuss what a company's responsibilities are to produce good products, to provide a good living for its employees, to help people, to make a lot of money for its shareholders. Is this the same for all types of companies?

A poll conducted by the Massachusetts Institute of Technology in the U.S. found that 87% of people think the Internet is the most important electronic invention of the 20th century. Other answers were cell phones (6%), automated teller machines (4%), fax machines (2%), and answering machines (1%).

A. Read the sentences in order to understand the phrasal verbs in **bold.**

1. Genetic tests can help doctors **work out** a person's risk of developing certain types of cancer.

2. Research that is **carried out** in genetics has provided, over the past few decades, great advances in medical science.

3. **Working on** ways to control serious illnesses is the main objective of medical research.

4. Unfortunately, some medical research organizations have begun to **tighten up on** their permissions to share and use the results of their research.

5. Such positions could **lead to** serious problems for humankind.

6. The research companies could **put up** the cost of their vital knowledge.

7. If research companies continue to **engage in** these greedy policies, many lower income groups would be unable to afford access to the information they need.

8. It is important for members of the public to **speak out against** the unethical behavior of these medical research companies.

9. Some governments **are looking into** ways of ensuring a fair deal both for the research companies and members of the public.

10. In the meantime, medical research companies **are pushing ahead with** this vital area of research.

B. Work with a partner. Rewrite sentences 1–10 in exercise A, replacing the phrasal verbs with the correct form of one of these synonyms.

study	do
cause	protest
continue with	examine
limit	increase
understand	pursue

C. Work alone and complete these statements with true information. Then work with a partner and ask one another questions about your beliefs or positions. Tell the class what you learn about your partner.

1. Our government should tighten up on _____.

2. I often speak out against _____.

3. We need to carry out more research into _____.

4. I can never understand why _____.

5. I personally would like to look into ways of _____.

D. Circle the verb that does not collocate with the *noun.*

1. do, carry out, make, perform *research*

2. have, follow, put, pursue *a dream*

3. cause, conduct, construct, carry out *a test*

4. examine, analyze, question, paint *the results*

5. develop, create, propose, dream *a theory*

Listening to instructions

Not all of the information in a talk or a conversation is equally important. When listening to instructions, think about the information you need, so that you concentrate more on the important parts and take less notice of the rest.

Before you listen

A. PAIR WORK Discuss the following questions with a partner. When you buy a new electronic gadget, how do you learn how to use it? Do you read the directions, ask someone what to do, or figure it out yourself? Does your method work well? Why or why not?

First listening

B. You are going to listen to a conversation between two friends. One of them has just bought a new computer printer. Write down all the words you hear that are related to computers.

Second listening

C. Listen again and number the pictures to show the correct sequence of steps in connecting the printer. One picture does not have a number.

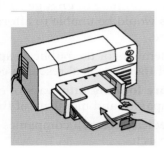

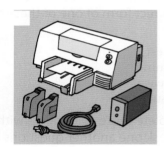
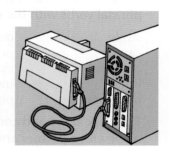

After listening

D. Which is the easiest way for you to follow directions—by looking at pictures, by reading instructions, or by listening to an explanation? Is this the same for everyone?

Test yourself

E. Read the questions, then listen and answer them. Try to ignore any information that is not related to the questions.

1. Where would you probably hear this talk?
   a. in a store   **b.** in a college   **c.** in a factory   **d.** in an office
2. What is the last step in sending a fax with this machine?
   a. enter the number of pages   **b.** press START   **c.** enter the fax number
   d. put in your document

Writing introductory paragraphs

Before you write

A. You are going to learn to write introductory paragraphs—that is, paragraphs that come at the beginning of a longer text, such as an essay or an article. In groups, discuss this list of items and decide which you would expect to find in an introductory paragraph. Give reasons for your decisions.

1. Specific arguments for or against the topic of the essay.
2. A sentence stating what the main focus of the essay will be.
3. At least one preamble sentence.
4. A justification for the choice of topic for the essay.
5. A statement (or statements) that sums up the main ideas discussed in the essay.
6. Detailed descriptions of certain aspects of the topic.

B. Reorder sentences 1–5 into a coherent introductory paragraph.

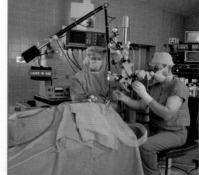

1. The Department of Oncology at the University of Kansas has set up several remote clinics.
2. The Kansas model has been so successful that many other states have implemented the same technology.
3. Not all news from the world of medicine is as grim as that from genetic testing.
4. Telemedicine procedures are very easy for both patients and medical staff to follow.
5. In remote areas of Kansas in the U.S., for example, sick people who can only be reached quickly by plane are benefiting greatly from telemedicine.

C. Do the same with these sentences for the introductory paragraph of an essay on the topic of rain forest conservation.

1. The loss negatively affects the balance in the world's ecology.
2. It is, therefore, urgent that world governments prevent further destruction of the forests.
3. Every year all over the world millions of kilometers of rain forest are lost.
4. In certain regions of the world, rain forest conservation projects have already been very successful, so a detailed examination of these is paramount.
5. This, in turn, has disastrous climatic consequences.

Write

D. Choose one of the following topic sentences and write a suitable introductory paragraph for an article or essay.

International tourism is causing major damage to the environment. *(newspaper article)*

There are many matters that are more urgent than environmental issues. *(essay)*

The world was a better place without the World Wide Web. *(essay)*

How we can solve the problem of genetic patents? *(newspaper article)*

A. Think of something funny that happened to you in the past. Make some notes of the main facts. Join a classmate and tell each other your story. Try to use reduced adverb clauses where appropriate.

EXAMPLE:

Notes:
Went out for lunch with my children last week
Ordered our meal
Sat there
Talked happily
Meal arrived
Requested catsup and mustard
My son was very hungry
Took the mustard container really quickly
Squeezed it but forgot to turn it downwards
Heard lots of laughter from the other tables
Turned and looked at my son
Hair and face covered in mustard

Story:
My children and I went out for lunch last week. After ordering our meal, we sat there, talking happily. When the meal arrived, we requested catsup and mustard. Being very hungry, my son took the mustard container really quickly and squeezed it, forgetting to turn it downwards. Hearing lots of laughter from the other tables, I turned and looked at my son. All I could see was this poor kid with his hair and face covered in mustard.

B. Think about something you have done in your life that required a lot of effort and sacrifice. Make notes of the main facts. Join a group of four and listen to one another's stories. Don't forget to use idiomatic expressions and phrasal verbs. Choose the best story in the group and ask the person who told that story to tell it to the whole class.

C. CLASS TASK Organize a debate on the topic below.

Medical research companies and big pharmaceutical companies should not be allowed to patent genes.

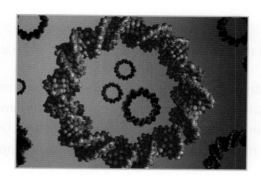

For more detail about Innovations, view the CNN video. Activities to accompany the video begin on page 142.

Business

1 Warm Up

A. In groups, describe what you see in each picture and discuss what all of the pictures have in common. Talk about whether or not you like the foods shown. Then brainstorm for the brand names of big companies you know whose main products are chocolate based. Talk about the kind of chocolate they produce and whether you like it or not.

B. Complete the sentences with one of the words or expressions from the box.

> stock market   shares   products   capital   sales   market research
> profit   market

1. Before setting up a business, you have to think carefully about the _____ you are going to sell.

2. A good way to find out whether your product will be successful or not is to do some _____ _____.

3. Making sure you have enough _____ to keep the business running for the first year is also very important.

4. It often takes some time before a business starts to make a _____.

5. Expect _____ to be quite slow initially as it takes time for people to become familiar with your product.

6. Once you have secured your _____, however, things will get gradually easier.

7. Before long your company might even be able to be listed on the _____ _____.

8. People are always looking for reliable companies in which they can invest by buying stocks and _____.

C. Brainstorm for the names of the major industries in your country. Then talk about where they operate and say whether you believe the presence of the industries has made a positive contribution to the development of the region in which they are situated.

Before you read

A. Discuss which industries you associate with these cities: Detroit, Hollywood, Seoul. Then brainstorm for other products and cities that are closely associated.

First reading

B. Scan the text and decide if these statements are True *(T)* or False *(F)*. Correct the false ones, and identify the information in the text that supports the true ones.

1. In general, people in the town of Hershey, Pennsylvania, believe that the sale of the Hershey Chocolate Company will have many advantages for them. _____
2. Other food companies in the U.S. have had to take decisions similar to those of Hershey. _____
3. Hershey is called Chocolate Town because its inhabitants eat a lot of chocolate. _____
4. The Hershey company was so successful that it was even productive during the Depression. _____
5. Milton Hershey founded the Milton Hershey School so that his children could get a good education. _____
6. Uncertainty in the stock market has forced Hershey trustees to diversify.
7. Hershey employees went on strike to get higher wages. _____
8. Lots of companies will want to buy Hershey because it is in Pennsylvania. _____

Reading strategy

Identifying the source of a text

When a text appears in a specific publication, its writer assumes that the reader has some knowledge or at least an interest in that field. For example, a gardeners' magazine assumes that its readers know something about gardening. Before you read an authentic text, notice its source and think about what the writer may assume you know.

Chocolate Town

The news this week that America's biggest chocolate company was to be sold by its controlling trust° was a personal **blow** to many of its employees. "It's a shock," said one employee. "It will hurt the community." She
5 sees the sale of the 108-year-old company as betraying° the memory of Milton Hershey, the businessman-philanthropist who **founded** Hershey and the town around it. "Milton Hershey would be very disappointed with what is happening. He was a man who gave his
10 employees the best he could."

The Hershey sale is not just another huge deal in a two-year wave of consolidation that has **reshaped** the U.S. food industry. It marks the loss of independence of one of America's oldest brands, with a huge potential
15 impact on the community it has supported for a century. It is also, in part, a **symptom** of the uncertainty and stock market volatility° that have followed the bursting° of the technology bubble.°

If Detroit is America's "Motor Town" and Pittsburgh
20 is its "Steel Town," Hershey, a factory town in Pennsylvania's rural Bethlehem Valley, is "Chocolate Town." On the main street, Chocolate
25 Avenue, the smell of the town's famous product fills the air. The street lamps are shaped like Hershey Kisses, the company's **signature** chocolate drops **launched** in 1907. Other streets, laid
30 out by Milton Hershey himself, have names such as Cocoa Avenue and Caracas Avenue—named for a main source of cacao beans. The town styles itself "The Sweetest Place on Earth."

Milton Hershey, born in 1857 and still widely
35 referred to by workers as Uncle Milt (fifty-seven years after his death), was descended from German and Dutch immigrants to Pennsylvania. Raised in a religion that stresses help for the poor and needy, Hershey became a sweet-maker and began building his
40 chocolate business in 1894. Like other chocolate entrepreneurs of that **era,** however, he built not just a factory but a town, in this case, a "Chocolate Town." It

had a park, a theater, and a golf course for workers. Hershey's business became a U.S. success story,
45 providing employment through the Depression, its product marketed as the "Great American Chocolate Bar."

The project closest to Hershey's heart, however, was the Milton Hershey School, founded in 1909 as a home for orphaned° boys, after he and his wife found that they
50 could not have children. On his wife's death, he endowed° the school with all his Hershey Chocolate Company stock. It is to protect the future **funding** of the school—which now welcomes all kinds of poor and disadvantaged children and is building new dormitories
55 to increase its capacity from 1,200 to 1,500—that the Milton Hershey School Trust is exploring a sale of its controlling stake in what is now Hershey Foods. The recent stock market slide and U.S. corporate **collapses** have only emphasized the risk for the trust, which has
60 been seeking to diversify for some time, of having 52% of its assets in one stock, even if it is Hershey. Hershey trustees believe that Milton Hershey would have approved of their decision as he gave up all his assets, including his home, to the trust to fund the school.
65 The sale decision is, however, another psychological blow to Hershey employees only just getting over a **bruising** strike° six weeks ago, Hershey's first in twenty-two years. The action was **triggered by** the efforts of Hershey's Chief Executive, the first outsider to occupy
70 this position, to cut costs by making employees

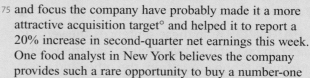

contribute more to their health insurance.° The Chief Executive's efforts to **streamline**
75 and focus the company have probably made it a more attractive acquisition target° and helped it to report a 20% increase in second-quarter net earnings this week. One food analyst in New York believes the company provides such a rare opportunity to buy a number-one
80 brand that a **bidding** war is likely. "This is an **iconic** American brand. Hershey has dominance of a big market," he claimed. "But while I'm all in favor of food industry consolidation, Milton Hershey must be rolling in his grave."

(Abridged from "Chocolate Town Goes up for Sale" by Neil Buckley and Ien Cheng, *Financial Times*, weekend of July 27/July 28, 2002.)

---

trust = organization with legal powers to take care of someone's property
betraying = not being true to, being disloyal to
volatility = unpredictability
bursting of a bubble = dramatic end to a period of rapid economic growth
orphaned = not having parents
endowed = provided for the permanent economic support
strike = when workers refuse to work for a specific reason
insurance = protection against damage or loss
acquisition target = investment

Second reading

C. Complete the summary with information from the reading.

Hershey, one of the most successful **(1)** _____, is to be sold. The Hershey controlling trust has taken this decision because of **(2)** _____ _____ _____ and because Hershey Foods **(3)** _____ in one stock, namely Hershey. The trust wishes to ensure that there will be sufficient **(4)** _____ for expansion at **(5)** _____, founded by Milton Hershey and very close to his heart. Based in a town of the same name, where everything **(6)** _____ you of chocolate, Hershey has been a source of **(7)** _____ for **(8)** _____ for over a century. While Hershey employees are worried that the sale of Hershey could mean **(9)** _____ , the stock market is excited about the sale of **(10)** _____.

Vocabulary in context

D. Find in the text a word or expression in **bold** that has the same or a similar meaning to the words and expressions in the list.

1. started very suddenly
2. old, well-known, and deserving of great respect
3. damaging
4. make more efficient
5. major disappointment
6. a period of history with a distinct character
7. means of identification, symbol
8. sudden loss of strength
9. established
10. changed completely
11. the money required for a project
12. sold or marketed for the first time
13. an indication
14. offer a price for the purchase of something

Discussion

E. Brainstorm for the names of any big companies that have provided employment for a lot of people in your country. Give examples that show that they have been good or bad employers.

Causative verbs

Passive causative constructions

Practice

A. PAIR WORK In these sentences, the verbs in *italics* can be put into two groups. Determine what distinguishes one group from the other and write the verbs in two lists.

1. Uncertainty in the stock market *has forced* the Hershey controlling trust *to sell* the company.

2. Although Milton Hershey *expected* his workers *to work* hard, he also gave them the best he could.

3. The new Hershey director became unpopular by trying to *make* employees *contribute* more to their health insurance.

4. Some religions *encourage* their followers *to be* sensitive to the needs of others.

5. Milton Hershey's parents never *let* him *forget* how important it was to help the poor.

6. Through strike action, workers can often *persuade* their employers not *to pursue* certain policies.

7. When they realized they could not have children, the Hersheys founded the Milton Hershey School to *help* them *forget* about their own disappointment.

8. When the stock market was strong in the late 1990s, many financial advisors *got* their customers *to invest* heavily.

9. Today the stock market is weak, so many investors will *ask* their advisors *to review* their investments.

10. My friend *had* his advisor *check out* her stock, and she was horrified to discover how much money she had lost.

B. Combine the pairs of sentences into one, omitting any parts that are no longer necessary and using the verbs in brackets.

EXAMPLE:
> *Monica bought some shares of stock. Her friend said it was a good idea.* (persuade)
> Monica's friend persuaded her to buy some shares of stock.
> *or*
> Monica bought some shares of stock because her friend persuaded her to.

1. George took guitar lessons. His father encouraged him. *(encourage)*

2. I went on a diet. My doctor believed it was necessary. *(get)*

3. I repeated my answer. This was the teacher's request. *(ask)*

4. His employees built Chocolate Town. Milton Hershey helped them. *(help)*

5. I gave up chocolate. My doctor thought it was bad for me. *(made)*

6. Jane didn't go on the trip. Her parents didn't like the idea. *(let)*

C. First work alone and complete these statements with true information. Then work with a partner and exchange information. Share what you learn about each other with the class.

1. When I lived with my parents, they made me _____.

2. I am very grateful to _____ because he / she encouraged me to _____.

3. It is never difficult to persuade me to _____.

4. When I am tired, I get my _____ to _____.

5. _____ helps me forget about my problems.

D. Study the examples. Then circle the correct answer in the notes about causative verbs with passive construction.

EXAMPLES:
> *I had my daughter picked up at 1 p.m. today.*
> *They got their car fixed before they sold it.*
> *She has a large cup of coffee brought to her office every morning.*
> *We'll get that letter rewritten tomorrow.*

1. In passive constructions with *have* and *get*, the second verb is in the *(simple past tense / past participle form)*.

2. The agent of the second verb is very *(important / not so important)*.

3. The second verb form in this construction always comes *(before / after)* the direct object.

4. "To" *(is used / is not used)* with the second verb form.

Causative verbs	Examples
A causative verb is the first verb in a statement that indicates the subject of the first verb influences other people to do something. In the active voice, the second verb is in the infinitive form.	*He asked* me *to leave* the room.
(a) Some causative verbs require the use of *to* with the second verb / infinitive form. **(b)** Others do not require *to*.	**a.** They *encouraged us to stay* longer. **b.** The police *made me show* them my driving license.
The direct object in these constructions is the doer of the action of the second verb.	They persuaded *me* to sell my car. (I sold my car because they thought it was a good idea.)
The second verb in these constructions uses the passive voice, especially the verbs *have* and *get*, to emphasize the action in the second verb and to take the focus off the agent.	I *had* my hair *cut*. (I made a decision about my hair. Someone cut it, but the identity of the person is not important.)

E. Respond to the comments.

EXAMPLE:
"These windows are dirty." (clean)
"Yeah. I must have <u>them cleaned</u>."

1. "The name on this passport looks strange." *(check)* "I'll get _____ tomorrow."
2. "The letters have been written." *(mail)* "Great! My secretary will have _____ tonight."
3. "Paul is stuck at the airport." *(send)* "Okay, we can arrange to have a car _____ to collect him right away."
4. "So what about the problem with your credit card?" *(refund)* "It's okay. I got the money _____ by my insurance company."

Test yourself

F. Complete the text with the correct form and tense of the verb in brackets. Where the verb in brackets is in the infinitive form, decide whether or not you need to add *to*.

When you set up a business, it is a good idea to **(1)** _____ *(have)* some market research **(2)** _____*(do)* before you **(3)** _____ *(start)*. You should also make sure that you **(4)** _____ *(have)* enough capital to see you through the barren period when there **(5)** _____ *(be)* no profits. **(6)** _____ *(get)* your bank manager **(7)** _____ *(help)* you check this out. Be sensible. If your bank manager **(8)** _____ *(ask)* you not **(9)** _____ *(be)* so ambitious, listen to him. Also, be careful with salespeople who try to persuade you **(10)** _____ *(buy)* all kinds of fancy things for your new office. You don't need them—at least not immediately. Once you have gotten the business **(11)** _____ *(organize),* you can concentrate on encouraging as many of your friends as possible **(12)** _____ *(buy)* your product and tell other people about it.

Paraphrasing to check understanding

A good way to check whether you understood another person's idea is by paraphrasing it—repeating it in your own words. Some expressions you can use:

So, you're saying that…
Let me see if I got that. You said…
So, you think…Is that right?

A. PAIR WORK Discuss. Do you know people who are self-employed or have their own business? What kinds of people like to start a business? Would you rather work for a boss or have your own business? What are the advantages and disadvantages of each option? If your partner makes a complicated statement, paraphrase it with one of the expressions from the Speaking focus box to see if you understood.

B. GROUP WORK Imagine that the members of your group have decided to start a business. Talk about group members' abilities and interests and decide what kind of business you will have. You can have a store, manufacture a product, provide a service, or do any other kind of business. Work together to produce a business plan, which you will present to the class as a report. Your business plan needs to cover the points below. When all groups have finished, take turns presenting your business plans to the class.

> the name of your business
> what you will sell, produce, or do for your customers
> the location of your business
> the job of each member of the group
> why your business will be unique or special
> why your business will be successful

There are about 200 million small businesses in the world today. In the U.K., the majority of businesses have fewer than fifty employees. There are 21 million small businesses in the U.S. and 2.3 million in Canada that have employees. But even more small businesses don't have any employees—only the owner.

C. CLASS TASK Discuss which of the businesses presented you think would be successful. Why? What factors are important in starting a new business? Do you think you would be a good entrepreneur?

A. Read the sentences to understand the phrasal verbs in **bold.** Then match each of the phrasal verbs with a word or expression from the box.

> become join sell well increase quickly employ
> stop working go out of business start

1. Before you **set up** a business, you need to think carefully about your product.
2. Market research can tell you if the product will **catch on** or not.
3. Often, as your business becomes successful, other businesses offer to **team up with** you.
4. The advantage of such an arrangement is that your business may **turn into** a big, powerful company.
5. The bigger your company is, the more workers you will have to **take on.**
6. Managing workers is not easy, especially if they favor strike action as opposed to negotiation and simply **walk out** in protest at some aspect of their working conditions.
7. If, however, you succeed in establishing a good relationship with your workers, your business is likely to prosper, and your stock market value will **shoot up.**
8. Patience and good planning usually prevent a business from losing money and eventually having to **close down.**

B. Make a coherent report on a business by circling the correct expression.

1. Good management has meant a sharp *(increase / decrease)* in our profits this year.
2. The fact that we set ourselves *(crazy / realistic)* sales targets has contributed to this.
3. We also *(kept within our budget / overspent on our budget).*
4. In contrast to us, the Whopper Chocolate Company has *(made a huge profit / made a huge loss).*
5. They launched *(a vast selection / a limited number)* of new products, which simply confused potential customers.
6. As a result, their shareholders are *(delighted / furious).*

C. Circle the adjective that does not collocate with the *noun.*

1. a sharp, steady, marginal, delightful, dramatic *increase*
2. a family, dramatic, booming, successful *business*
3. a marginal, disappointing, encouraging, predictable *trend*
4. a parent, cousin, multinational, limited *company*
5. realistic, achievable, unrealistic, steep *targets*

> **FYI**
> A collocation is the result of two words that are commonly used together, especially adjectives and nouns.

Listening strategy

Noticing format

Certain types of information that we listen to are presented in standard formats. For example, train departures and arrivals are announced according to an established formula. The prerecorded messages we hear on calling a business are another case. Think about the style of these announcements and messages before you listen and this will help you understand the information more easily.

Before you listen

A. If you need information from a store or business, how do you usually get it? Do you go there, phone, or search online? What are the advantages and disadvantages of each option?

First listening

B. Listen to the three recorded telephone messages. What kind of business is each message for?

Message 1: _____
Message 2: _____
Message 3: _____

Second listening

C. For each message, read the situation and then listen again to find out what the caller should do.

Message 1: You want to talk to a customer service representative.

Message 2: There is a mistake in your bill.

Message 3: You want to go to London.

After listening

D. Which is better for a business—an employee answering the phone or a recorded message? Which is better for customers? Why?

Test yourself

E. Look at the question and think about the format you might expect to hear. Then listen to the recording and answer the question.

You are looking for a pharmacy that is open on Sunday. What should you do?

a. stay on the line   **b.** press *   **c.** press 1   **d.** press 2

Writing the introductory paragraph of a business letter

Before you write

A. GROUP WORK Discuss whether or not these expressions would be appropriate in a business letter. Give reasons for your decisions.

Dear Paul Robertson
Hi Paul
Dear Mr. Robertson
Hello Paul
Dear Paul

Can't wait to meet you
Am looking forward to meeting you
About that order you placed the
    other day
With reference to your recent order
Might take a bit of time to ship it
    to you
I will inform you of the progress
    we make on this matter at the
    earliest opportunity

So long!
See you soon
Bye for now
Sincerely
Yours sincerely

B. Reorganize the sentences in the model letter to make the introductory paragraph of a letter from a big company to its shareholders. Discuss with your group which of the sentences tells the reader about the direction the letter is going to take after the first paragraph.

Write

C. Write an introductory paragraph for a business letter based on one of the situations. Then join someone who chose a different topic from yours and read each other's letters. Make suggestions for improvements if necessary.

- To the employees of a factory: The factory is going to close down because it has run into serious financial problems.

- To the employees of a factory: The factory has made record profits, and as a result, major improvements will be made to working conditions and wages.

- To the shareholders of a large company: Shares have not made very good earnings over the past financial year.

Star Foods Inc.

January 2003

Dear Shareholders:

Re: The past year and the years to come

a. The year began badly after one of the worst Christmas periods ever with consumer spending at its lowest for years.
b. You will, therefore, be pleased to note that, despite the international turmoil and the slump in the stock markets, Chocolate Serene has made modest but steady progress in both sales and earnings.
c. This was compounded by instability in the stock markets caused by international tensions and a threat of war.
d. Chocolate Serene's tradition of careful planning and its previous experience with bad patches in the market, however, has made it a very resilient company.
e. As you are probably aware, last year was a major challenge for all kinds of businesses—large and small alike.

A. GROUP WORK Imagine you are on the board of directors of a big business that was booming for many years but is now not doing well.

- Decide what your line of business is and give it a name.
- Discuss all the reasons why your business did so well for many years.
- List all the reasons why your business is not doing so well now.
- Write a six- to eight-point plan that you will follow to save your business from closing down. Use causative verbs such as: *request, ask, get, have, help, make, force, let, allow.*

EXAMPLES:

Reduce secretarial costs by getting junior executives to deal with their own correspondence.
Make all employees stick more rigidly to office and factory schedules.
Ask market research company to . . .

B. Imagine you have just inherited or won a very large amount of money, which means you can now pay other people to do things you don't like to do or that you do badly. List five things you hate to do and five you do badly. Then, under each item on your list, indicate a possible solution. Work in pairs and tell one another what you wrote. Then tell the class what you have learned about your partner.

EXAMPLE:

Things I hate to do	***Things I do badly***
my accounts	*painting and decorating*

SOLUTION:

employ an accountant to do them	*buy a new house or pay a friend to redecorate*

C. CLASS TASK Hold a debate on this topic:

There is no such thing as a truly philanthropic business person.

For more detail about Business, view the CNN video. Activities to accompany the video begin on page 142.

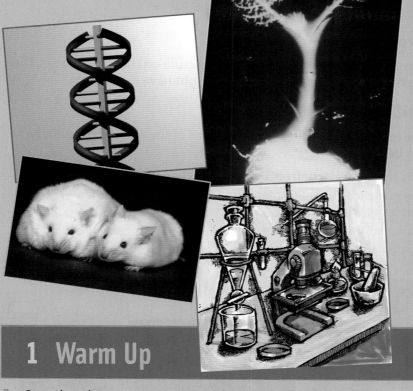

Research

Communication

Discussing animal rights and
   scientific research

Debating how governments
   should use their resources

Guidelines for oral presentations

Grammar

Consolidation: the indefinite,
   definite, and zero articles

Vocabulary

Review of the use of the suffix
   -less

Phrasal verbs used in reports

Scientific lexis: common
   derivations

Skills

Skimming scientific texts

Listening for arguments

Writing: text with an
   introductory and supporting
   paragraph

1 Warm Up

A. Say what these acronyms stand for. Then discuss when and in what ways each of these research discoveries became important for humankind.

    DNA   GM   IVF   AI

B. Work in groups and match the words on the left with their meanings on the right.

1. to implant
2. to fertilize
3. to fragment
4. to protest
5. to preserve
6. to resurrect

   a. divide, break into bits and pieces
   b. complain about something, say
       something is wrong or unfair
   c. put into (a living organism)
   d. bring back to life
   e. start the development of a new life
   f. maintain in good condition

C. Use derivations of the words in exercise B to complete the chart.

Verb	Noun (person, agent, object)	Adjective	Noun (process)
1. to implant	implant		_____
2. to fertilize	_____	fertilized	fertilization
3. to fragment		fragmentary	_____
4. to protest	_____ _____		_____
5. to preserve	a preservative	preserved	_____
6. to resurrect		_____	_____

Reading strategy

Looking for connectors

Discursive texts often contain words and phrases that lead the reader through the arguments the writer wishes to put forward. Words like *therefore, however, but*, etc., give us clues as to what comes next. Spotting these signals will help you to understand a text more easily.

FYI

U.S. ton = 2,000 pounds
U.K. ton = 2,240 pounds
tonne (metric ton) = 1,000 kilos (2,204.62 pounds)

Before you read

A. In groups, describe what you see in each picture on these two pages. Then talk about what the subjects of the pictures might have in common.

First reading

B. Skim the reading and decide which sections of the reading go with the descriptions below.

1. indicates that tighter controls are needed when tinkering with nature ___
2. provides evidence that poor planning can be a problem when experimenting with nature ___
3. paints a hopeful picture of experiments with nature ___
4. has a happy ending ___

Refining Research

Introduction

Fiery debates, like those surrounding the cloning of human embryos, have accompanied advances in scientific research ever since humans began
5 experimenting with nature. Young people today might be surprised to learn, for instance, that the invention of IVF°, now a routine **procedure** that solves the problem of childlessness for thousands of couples, was initially greeted, in many societies, with stormy protests from
10 certain pressure groups.° As scientists **refine** their understanding of the new inventions and become more successful with their applications, however, there is a tendency for their use to be accepted as **inevitable** and for the controversial debates to subside. As the following
15 sections show, therefore, the real concern is not so much about the potential benefits of scientific discoveries but about the thorough planning and **stringent** control of how and when they are applied.

Possum Problems

20 Introduced into New Zealand about two hundred years ago, this small, **furry** Australian animal was to be used in the creation of a fur industry. On removing the possum from its natural habitat, however, scientists forgot about its natural **predators**. With no
25 predators in New Zealand, the possum population in New Zealand has exploded° to more than 60 million and possum are now one of the country's biggest **pests**, gobbling up° 60,000 tonnes of vegetation a day. Ironically, it is recent advances in
30 science that might help solve the possum problem. New Zealand GM researchers are developing a carrot that expresses° a protein to disrupt° the reproductive system of the female possum.

Baby Blunder

35 In 1999, after IVF treatment, a white mother gave birth to "twins," but one of the baby boys was black and the other was white. The fertility clinic in the U.S. had accidentally implanted the white woman with a fertilized egg belonging to another woman, together
40 with one of her own. Both women had tried unsuccessfully for years to have children before attending the clinic, where, eventually, they received fertilized eggs on the same day. Subsequently, the black woman was devastated to discover that she was not
45 pregnant, while the white woman was delighted to be told that she was carrying twins. Before the babies were born, however, doctors had to break the news to her that she might be carrying the child of another

couple. DNA tests later confirmed that one of them was
50 not biologically related to her, but she went ahead with
the pregnancy. For three months after the birth, the white
mother refused to hand over the black baby to its
biological parents, who, meantime, had initiated a
custody battle. As the court case approached, however,
55 and after further DNA tests proved that the black baby
was indeed the child of that particular black couple, the
white couple handed over the baby. The white mother,
who had loved and regarded both babies as her own, was
torn apart by her decision but could not justify
60 **depriving** "her" son of being brought up by his
biological parents.

Crossing Camels
What do a llama and a camel have in common? Thirty
million years ago, both of these closely related species
65 lived together in North America. Now with the help of
AI, the two species have been **crossbred** to produce a
"cama." As with all crossbreeding projects, it is hoped
that the cama, a female born at the Camel Reproduction

Center in Dubai,
70 United Arab
Emirates, will be
stronger and more
productive than each
of the original
75 species and that she
will have **traits** that are common to both. For example,
researchers believe she will produce a high quality
fleece° and will be adaptable to different kinds of
climates.

IVF = in vitro fertilization
pressure groups = groups of people who try to influence public opinion and government action
exploded = increased very dramatically
gobbling up = eating quickly and voraciously
GM = genetic modification
expresses = contains (scientific term)
disrupts = causes disorder or malfunctioning
fleece = the woolly coat of certain animals like sheep and goats

---

Second reading

C. Read the text again. Then fill in the blanks in the paragraph with as many words or phrases as necessary for the paragraph to represent a summary of the text.

Research that experiments with humans and animals needs to be **(1)** _____ and **(2)** _____ in order to avoid **(3)** _____ like the one which was made with the possum in New Zealand. The possum was brought from **(4)** _____ to **(5)** _____ to be used in **(6)** _____, but scientists forgot about **(7)** _____ . As a result, the possum **(8)** _____ and is now **(9)** _____ in New Zealand because it **(10)** _____. Similarly, in the U.S., a white mother had **(11)** _____ and eventually **(12)** _____ produced one black and one white baby because the fertility clinic **(13)** _____ . If, however, these kinds of treatments based on research are well planned and tightly controlled, they can **(14)** _____. For example, thanks to AI (artificial insemination), scientists in Dubai, by **(15)** _____ with a camel have created **(16)** _____, which _____.

Vocabulary in context

D. Find words or phrases in **bold** in the text with a similar meaning to those below.

1. detailed method for doing something
2. produce offspring from two different plants or animal
3. devastated
4. characteristics or qualities
5. animals that survive by killing other animals
6. passionate or full of feeling
7. make better or improve
8. prevent from having
9. extremely strict
10. certain to happen
11. with a thick, hairy coat
12. small animals or insects that cause damage to food or plants

Discussion

E. Discuss any experiments with animals or humans similar to those in the text that you have heard about. Give reasons why you believe the experiments were or were not successful.

Consolidation: the indefinite, definite, and zero articles

Practice

A. Read these four sentences below and underline the option that explains how the articles are used.

1. IVF is **a** routine procedure that, in some cases, helps couples solve **the** problem of childlessness.

   The indefinite article **a** is used to classify OR The indefinite article **a** is used to generalize *routine procedure*.

   The definite article **the** is used to classify *problem*. OR The definite article **the** is used because *problem* is limited or identified with the expression *of childlessness*.

2. As **ø** scientists refine their understanding of **the** new inventions and become more successful with their applications, however, there is **a** tendency for their use to be accepted as inevitable

   There is a zero article (**ø**) before *scientists* because *scientists* is in the plural OR There is a zero article (**ø**) before *scientists* because this is a generalization about all scientists.

   The definite article **the** is used before *new inventions* because the inventions have been mentioned before OR The definite article **the** is used because the inventions are new.

   The indefinite article **a** is used before *tendency* because it is singular OR The indefinite article **a** is used to classify *tendency*.

3. What is the difference between **a** llama and **a** camel?

   The indefinite article **a** is used before *llama* and *camel* because both nouns are singular OR The indefinite article **a** is used before *llama* and *camel* because the use is generic, i.e., both nouns are being used to refer to each and all the representations of llamas and camels as a whole.

4. **ø** New Zealand GM researchers are developing **a** carrot that expresses a protein that disrupts **the** reproductive system of **the** female possum.

   There is a zero article (**ø**) before *researchers* because it is the first time they are mentioned OR There is a zero article (**ø**) before *researchers* because all GM researchers in New Zealand are involved in the project.

   The indefinite article **a** is used with *carrot* to show that the carrot belongs in a specific class

OR The indefinite article **a** is used to count the carrot.

The definite article **the** is used with *reproductive system* because female animals have only one reproductive system OR The definite article **the** is used because the reproductive system was mentioned before.

The definite article **the** is used with *possum* because the use is generic, i.e., to refer to the entire class of possums as a whole (sometimes this use and example 3 are interchangeable. See grammar chart) OR The definite article **the** is used because possums have been mentioned before.

B. Re-read the text below and try to explain the choice of articles in each case.

Introduced into **ø** New Zealand about two hundred years ago, this small, furry Australian animal was to be used in **the** creation of **a** fur industry. On removing **the** possum from its natural habitat, however, **ø** scientists forgot about its natural predators. With no predators in New Zealand, **the** possum population in New Zealand has exploded to more than 60 million and **ø** possum are now one of **the** country's biggest pests, gobbling up 60,000 tonnes of vegetation a day. Ironically, it is **ø** recent advances in **ø** science that might help solve **the** possum problem.

C. PAIR WORK Complete these sentences with information about your country. Decide which article (zero, definite, or indefinite) you need. Then work with a partner to compare and refine your answers. Share your answers with the class.

1. _____ is the most beautiful building in our country.

2. _____ and _____ are the fruits that people eat most in our country.

3. _____ is a beautiful flower that grows in our country.

4. _____ president / prime minister of our country is called _____.

5. _____ name of my favorite musician from our country is _____.

6. _____ is a musical instrument. It is typical of our country.

7. The capital of our country is _____. It is _____ very busy city.

Consolidation: the indefinite, definite, and zero articles

Main uses of the indefinite article *a/an*	Examples
1. to classify a singular noun, showing that it belongs in a class or group	**1.** *This is a piano.*
2. a. in a nonspecific sense to mean "any one" of a kind **b.** in an enumerative use of *a* to mean "one"	**2. a.** *What would you like? An apple or an orange?* (You may have any apple or orange of the ones I have on offer.) **b.** *I'd like an apple, an orange, and two bananas, please.* (an = one)
3. with singular concrete generic nouns to express generalized instances of that noun	**3.** *A kangaroo carries its baby in its pouch.* **Note:** This use does not represent the class as a whole (See 8a below) and may alternately be written: *The kangaroo carries its baby in its pouch.*

Main uses of the definite article *the*	Examples
4. with unique nouns	**4. a.** *The brain is the most important organ in the human body.* **b.** *The Charles Bridge in Prague is very old.*
5. to identify	**5.** *Look! That's the restaurant I told you about.*
6. to talk about something already mentioned	**6.** *There is a beautiful mountain in Japan. The mountain is called Mount Fuji.*
7. when the noun is followed by a modifying "of" phrase	**7.** *IVF has helped many couples with the problem of childlessness.*
8. generically to refer to an entire class of humans, animals, organs of the body, plants and complex inventions and devices	**8. a.** *The possum was removed to New Zealand.* **Note:** This cannot be replaced by *A possum was removed to New Zealand.* **b.** *Many people in Latin America play the guitar.*
9. when what you are talking about can be seen or heard by the speakers	**9.** *That's the telephone.*

Main uses of the zero (ø) article	Examples
10. with plural nouns that have a general focus	**10.** *ø Elderly people should be respected.*
11. with noncount and abstract nouns that are unspecified	**11. a.** *I need to buy ø tea and ø sugar.* **b.** *All they need is ø love.* Contrast: *I need to buy the tea you recommended.* *The love of one's family is essential for normal development.*
12. with the names of most cities, countries, and continents unless *the* is part of the name	**12. a.** *Seoul is a big, busy, dynamic city.* **b.** *The Hague is my favorite European city.*

Test yourself

D. In each sentence, circle the error(s) in the use of articles and then correct it.

1. Earth moves around sun.
2. The guitar is musical instrument that is very popular in Hispanic countries.
3. The Hiroshima is a city of peace and reconciliation.
4. Solar system consists of the sun, the planets, and their satellites.
5. In the interest of the progress, scientific experiments are necessary.
6. Kangaroo in the zoo near my house is pregnant.
7. Desert can be very beautiful but frightening place.
8. Tiger is an endangered species.

Speaking focus

Making a presentation

Here are some basic points to remember when you speak in front of an audience.

- Make eye contact with your audience. Look around at different people.
- Write short notes to help you remember important points, but don't read from your paper. Look at your notes only if you forget something.
- Speak a little bit louder than your normal voice, so that everyone can hear you.

A. PAIR WORK Discuss these questions in pairs. Are there any rare plants or animals in your country? Where do they live? Have you ever seen them?

B. GROUP WORK Work in groups of four. Imagine that you are a member of the City Council of Bigville. Your city is having a lot of problems with money. The schools are extremely crowded, and some classes have to meet in the hall. You have bought some land to build a large new school. But the week before construction is planned to begin, an environmental group announces that they have found rare plants everywhere on that land. The plants are an endangered species that grows only around your city, and they are very delicate. Many scientists believe that these plants contain a drug that could cure cancer. What should Bigville do? Below are different plans that have been proposed. Add your own plan, then discuss all the plans with your group and decide which is best.

1. **Plan 1:** Do nothing. Don't build the school. Don't do anything to the plants.
2. **Plan 2:** Build the school. Don't worry about the plants.
3. **Plan 3:** Built the school. Try to move the plants to another place.
4. **Plan 4:** Sell all the plants to a chemical company to get money for the city.
5. **Plan 5:** Don't build the school. Try to sell the land to get money to build in another place.
6. **Plan 6:** Express your own idea.
7. **Your plan:** _____

C. GROUP WORK Prepare a short presentation to give to the class. In your presentation, include answers to these questions.

Which plan did you choose?
What are the advantages of this plan?
What are the disadvantages of this plan?
What will be the outcome of following this plan?

D. CLASS TASK Take turns standing up in front of the class to give your group presentations. Remember the points in the Speaking focus box.

Indonesia is home to the greatest number of endangered species of mammals in the world, while the Philippines has the largest number of endangered bird species. Malaysia has the greatest number of endangered plant species—mostly rain forest trees.

5 Vocabulary in Detail

A. PAIR WORK Match the sentences on the left with the statements on the right. Then use the words in **bold** to talk about your own experiences.

EXAMPLE: *I bought a new cell phone last week, but it was **useless** so I took it back.*

1. Paul and Jane are **childless**.
2. Those employees are **careless** workers.
3. It's **hopeless**.
4. The person who did it shall be **nameless**.
5. In the end it was a **fruitless** trip.
6. Calling him is **pointless**.
7. This gadget is **useless**.
8. **Doubtless** they will be at the party.

a. Throw it away!
b. Don't even try!
c. He won't change his mind.
d. They are very sociable.
e. They are going to try IVF.
f. They make a lot of mistakes.
g. We achieved nothing.
h. We don't wish to embarrass him or her.

B. Read the text and complete the phrasal expressions with one of the particles in the box.

up	to (3)	against	of	through	out	ahead with	about

A lot of modern scientific research *consists* **(1)** _____ experimenting with animals. Before *going* **(2)** _____ such research, however, most scientific organizations *weigh* the advantages of the research for humans **(3)** _____any harm it might do to the animals which they will *subject* **(4)** _____ experimentation. Often, members of the public become very *concerned* **(5)** _____ the rights of the animals and *resort* **(6)** _____ staging protests outside the offices of the organization. Usually, however, the scientific organizations have the full support of their government as they have proved that the experiments which they *carry* **(7)** _____ have *led* **(8)** _____ major improvements in the treatment of certain illnesses while not causing any harm to the animals. Often, too, meetings are organized between the scientists and the protesters and once the scientists *have gone* **(9)** _____ the details of the treatment the animals receive, the protesters *give* **(10)** _____ their campaigns.

C. PAIR WORK Find a one-word verb or another phrasal verb in this list with the same or a similar meaning to the phrasal verbs in exercise B.

1. result in
2. be made up of
3. start, begin
4. cause someone or something to experience
5. worry about
6. explain
7. stop
8. contrast with
9. do
10. use as an extreme solution

Listening strategy

Listen for arguments

When discussing a controversial topic, a speaker will often use arguments to try to make you agree with his or her opinion. Listen carefully for the arguments, which may or may not be good ones, and decide whether or not you agree with the speaker.

Before you listen

A. Discuss the following questions. What do you know about genes? Why are they important for plants and animals? Do you know about any recent genetic experiments? Do you think these experiments are a good idea?

B. You are going to listen to two speakers answering the question: *Should the government control genetic research?* After listening and taking notes, decide which speaker you agree with, and say why. What kind of information will you need to include in your notes?

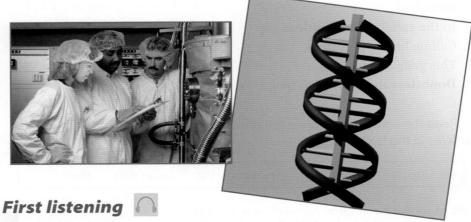

First listening

C. Divide your paper into two columns, one for each speaker. Listen and write down in your own words each speaker's main point.

Second listening

D. Listen again and take notes about the speakers' arguments in favor of their opinions.

After listening

E. Read through your notes and circle the arguments you agree with. If you disagree with a point, think of reasons why. Which speaker do you agree with and why? If you disagree with both speakers, explain your own opinion.

Test yourself

F. Listen to the speech and answer the questions.

1. What is the speaker's main point?
   a. Scientists should make decisions about science.
   b. We're spending too much money on useless research.
   c. Humans are changing the way nature works.
   d. Research on genes should be ended.

2. Which of the following is not an argument used by the speaker?
   a. People are using genetic discoveries for bad purposes.
   b. Humans are different from animals.
   c. We don't completely understand how genes work.
   d. Genetic research takes money away from more important uses.

Writing a text with an introductory and supporting paragraph

Before you write

A. GROUP WORK Read the text and select the correct answer to the questions. Discuss the reasons for your choices.

> Using robots in scientific research provides many advantages over using real animals. To begin with, they do not require feeding, watering, or special housing. They can easily be put away in a box or closet overnight or even be used twenty-four hours a day. They also have the advantage that, when scientists work with the artificial brains of robots, there are no ethical dilemmas or animal welfare issues to be considered. Perhaps the main advantage of robots, however, is that they are so much easier to control than real animals.

1. Where would you expect to find this type of text?
   a. a newspaper article **d.** an advertisement
   b. a business letter **e.** a company report
   c. an academic essay

2. Where does this paragraph belong?
   a. right at the beginning of **c.** at the very end of the
   the text text
   the text
   b. somewhere in the middle
   of the text

3. What does this paragraph do?
   a. describe something in detail **d.** discuss the pros and cons of
   b. narrate a sequence of events something
   c. explain what something is **e.** argue a case for (using) something
   or how it works

B. Order these sentences so that they form a coherent paragraph and decide how this paragraph relates to the one in exercise A.

1. Over the last few years, however, the focus of research has begun to change.
2. For example, in 1738 a French engineer, Jacques de Vaucanson, created one of the very first robots—a mechanical duck.
3. Instead of studying animals to help them build better robots, scientists are now studying robots to help them better understand animals.
4. Robot engineers have always looked to nature for inspiration.

Write

C. Choose one of the topics and write two paragraphs—an introductory paragraph and a supporting paragraph—to argue your case. Then find a partner who chose a different topic from yours. Read each other's paragraphs and help each other to refine your writing.

- against IVF
- in favor of GM crops
- in favor of the crossbreeding of two animals
- in favor of using animals in scientific research

A. PAIR WORK Choose a living creature and write brief notes on it using these headings.

Classification: e.g., *a mammal, bird, fish, insect, reptile, etc.*
Geographic location: e.g., *worldwide, African continent, etc.*
Description and name: e.g., *flat and some can fly, cockroach*

B. Join with another pair of students and take turns guessing. Use only Yes / No questions and try to guess what the living thing is using a maximum of ten questions. After you have asked some questions recap what you know.

EXAMPLE:
> *S1: Is it an insect?*
> *S2: Yes, it is.*
> *S3: Do we have them in our country?*
> *S4: Yes, we do.*
> *S3: Okay. So far, we know that it's an insect and we have them in our country.*

C. Each of these sentences is a well-known English proverb. With a partner, read each one and decide which article (*the, a/an, ø*) completes each blank. Be prepared to justify your choice. Then discuss the meanings of these proverbs and compare them with similar ones in your own language.

1. _____ absence makes _____ heart grow fonder.
2. When in _____ Rome, do as _____ Romans do.
3. Too many cooks spoil _____ broth.
4. Many hands make _____ light work.
5. _____ love makes _____ world go round.
6. _____ apple _____ day keeps _____ doctor away.
7. _____ time flies.
8. You can't teach _____ old dog _____ new tricks.
9. When _____ poverty comes in through _____ door, _____ love goes out through _____ window.
10. _____ money talks.

D. CLASS TASK Debate this topic.

Governments should spend more time and money on solving practical problems such as poverty, inadequate housing, and illiteracy and less on scientific research.

For more detail about Research, view the CNN video. Activities to accompany the video begin on page 143.

Review Your Grammar

A. Complete each sentence with the correct form of the verb in parentheses.

1. (eat) Don't let the dog _____ that chocolate bar!
2. (check) We had the veterinarian _____ the cat's ears.
3. (be) We expected the bill _____ about $20.
4. (pay) They made us _____ over $100.
5. (cut) My husband persuaded the vet _____ $10 from the bill.
6. (spend) Then the vet encouraged us _____ $25 to have the dog's teeth cleaned.

B. Fill in the blank with *a, an, the,* or *ø* to indicate the zero article.

1. Can you give me _____ aspirin for my headache?
2. I don't think that _____ snakes deserve such a bad reputation.
3. Would you like to borrow _____ dime? I have three or four in my purse.
4. Proper use of _____ tongue is a very important part of clear speech.
5. _____ young sometimes don't appreciate the value of life experience.
6. I hope to visit _____ Miami next winter.

High Challenge

C. Combine each pair of sentences using a reduced adverb clause.

EXAMPLE:

I live in New York City. I see a lot of Broadway plays.
<u>Living in New York City, I see a lot of Broadway plays.</u>

1. Carrie was feeling sad. She decided to visit her aunt.

_____

2. I didn't know Chinese. I couldn't order food in Beijing.

_____

3. Mary had lived for a long time in France. She spoke excellent French.

_____

4. All children love Disneyland. It is also fun for many adults.

_____

5. Pollution is usually found in big cities. It can also be found in small towns.

_____

Review Your Vocabulary

A. Match the words and phrases that mean the opposite.

___ **1.** volatile   **a.** generous
___ **2.** furious   **b.** pleased
___ **3.** radical   **c.** lazy
___ **4.** latent   **d.** conservative
___ **5.** greedy   **e.** visible
___ **6.** persevering   **f.** calm

B. Use words and expressions from the box to complete the conversation.

| based on   give up   speak out against   set up   refine   close down |

Nitza: I think we should **(1)** _____ the use of animals in laboratory experiments.
Otto: Well, maybe. But they can't **(2)** _____ all the labs doing animal experiments.
Nitza: Why not? Why can't they **(3)** _____ experiments without using animals?
Otto: The research on most new life-saving drugs is **(4)** _____ animal testing.
Nitza: Couldn't they **(5)** _____ the tests? Maybe they could find a way not to use animals.
Otto: You're not going to **(6)** _____ on this, are you?
Nitza: No, I'm not!

C. Unscramble the phrases below.

1. some up team with people _____

2. price increase a in sharp _____

3. volatile triggered a market by _____

4. miracle short nothing a of _____

5. plans ahead your push with _____

6. the bubble technology burst _____

FYI

In some tests you may need to complete a sentence with the correct form of a word. So it is useful to study word formation. This means examining all the grammatically different words, both positive and negative, that you can make from one word. For example, from the word *predict* we can form: *prediction, predictable, predictability, predictably, predictive, predictor, unpredictable,* and so on.

Review Your Speaking

Fluency

A. PAIR WORK Choose one of the inventions in the pictures and describe to your partner what it is and how this invention has benefited the world. Has it had any negative effects? If so, describe these also.

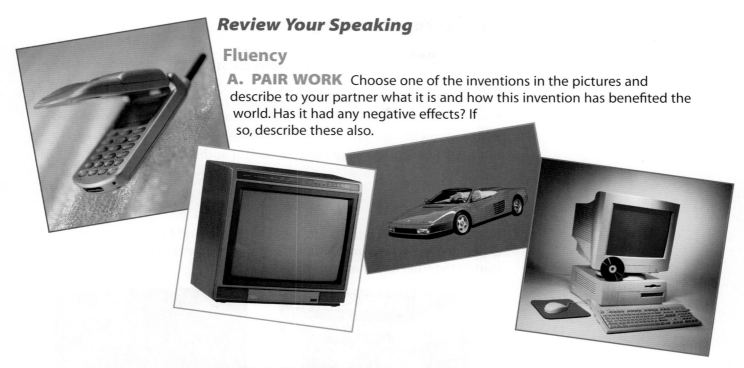

B. GROUP WORK You are going to give short presentations. Make notes below about an invention that you think would help people. Then tell your group about your idea. Remember to glance at (not read) your notes, to make eye contact, and to speak in a somewhat louder voice than usual.

What will the invention do?	
What will it look like?	
Who will the invention help?	
How will you put it together?	
How much will it cost?	

F•A•Q Sometimes when my teacher asks us to discuss a topic, I can't think of anything to say about it. What can I do?

A common type of approach at the advanced level of English is to focus on the advantages and disadvantages of the topic under discussion. To think of ideas, try to imagine someone who is very different from you—perhaps of a different generation, or the opposite sex—and how this person might feel about that topic. For example, if the topic is cellular phones, maybe you consider they are indispensable, but would your grandparents feel the same?

Review Your Listening

A. PAIR WORK Discuss the following questions.

- Do you know anyone who owns a business?
- What are some advantages and disadvantages of "being your own boss"?
- Would you like to start your own business? Why or why not?
- What kinds of people are most successful at this?

Listening 1

B. You are going to hear an interview with John and Delia Haynes, two experts on self-employment. Listen and find the name of the business they started together and the type of work it does.

C. Listen again and find five kinds of work they have done. You will need to ignore a lot of irrelevant information.

Listening 2

D. The second part of the interview tells listeners how to decide whether they could be successful business owners. Would you be successful? Listen and write down four qualities that are important.

E. Listen again and take notes on these qualities.

Upbringing

1 Warm Up

A. PAIR WORK Describe the pictures. Then discuss the kinds of
knowledge and skills the people who live and work in each environment
are likely to develop.

B. Complete the sentences with the correct form of the phrasal verbs in
the boxes.

1. Children who are **(a)** _____ _____ in a caring and supportive
   environment usually **(b)** _____ to be secure and happy adults.
   Although they may **(c)** _____ one or both of their parents in their
   physical characteristics, the environment in which they are raised
   will have a significant effect on their emotional development.

   > take after   bring up   grow up

2. When they **(a)** _____ major difficulties, knowing that they can
   (b) _____ the support of a loving family helps people **(c)** _____ the
   difficulties.

   > face up to   rely on   come up against

3. There are, however, always exceptions to the rule. Despite a
   supportive upbringing, some children **(a)** _____ unhappy and
   insecure adults who simply cannot **(b)** _____ even the smallest of
   problems. These people usually **(c)** _____ requesting help from
   trained professionals.

   > develop into   end up   deal with

C. With the class, talk about where and how you were brought up.
Discuss any specific knowledge, skills, or attitudes that you believe are a
direct result of that environment.

Comparing opinion with evidence

There are some topics on which you may have a strong personal opinion; for example, the topic of what has more influence on people—their upbringing or their genes. As you read, compare your opinion with the evidence offered in the reading. Be careful not to let your own opinion make you misinterpret a text.

Before you read

A. GROUP WORK Discuss which of these statements you agree with and which you do not agree with. Use your own life experiences to justify your opinions.

1. In the development of people's characters, the environment in which they are brought up plays a more significant role than their genes.
2. Everybody has certain hereditary traits that can never be changed, either by the environment or by a person's own efforts.
3. With the right motivation, you can achieve almost anything you want to in life.
4. Animals do not have emotions.
5. People who suffer deprivation in early childhood have serious emotional problems for the rest of their lives.

First reading

B. Scan the three readings and indicate which one or ones match the descriptions below.

1. shows the strong effect of the environment on people
2. is about a child and wild animals in Africa
3. indicates that nature has a strong effect on people's emotional makeup
4. is about two people in the U.S.
5. is about a child and animals in Europe

Life Histories

1. Gary Klahr 52 and Steven Barbin 49, both from Connecticut, met in a bar 28 years ago and immediately **hit it off.** They became close friends—so close that Klahr was best man at Barbin's wedding and once signed
5   a photograph "You are truly my brother." How truly, they had no idea.

Three years ago, a man contacted state officials in Connecticut **seeking** information from his adoption° file for medical reasons. He discovered that he was one of
10 nine, in a family of 13 children, whose parents had given them up for adoption. The case worker who **dug up** the records at the Department of Children and Families decided to contact the other
15 eight.

She called Klahr first. He was surprised to learn he was adopted, since the
20 couple who **raised** him had never told him. "I said, 'My best

friend was adopted and he's OK with it, so I guess I will be OK too,'" he recalled. It was then he discovered
25 that Barbin was in fact his brother, as was his gym work-out partner!

2. There are many stories of children who have been brought up by, or lived for long periods of time, with wild animals—for example, wolves, bears, and
30 monkeys. While some of these stories are **unproven,** others are known to be true. "In all my travels, the only time I ever slept deeply was when I was with wolves . . . The days of my wolf family multiplied. I have no idea how many months I spent with them but I wanted it to
35 last forever—it was far better than returning to the world of my own kind . . . Those were the most beautiful days I had ever experienced." So wrote Misha Defonseca, a Jewish orphan who, from the ages of seven to eleven, **wandered** through the woods° and
40 forests of Nazi-occupied Europe during WW2, living on wild **berries,** raw meat and food stolen from farmhouses, and occasionally **teaming up with** wolves. "Over time all my senses were **heightened**— my vision, my hearing, even my sense of smell," wrote
45 Defonseca. "That hypersensitivity° stayed with me for a very long time after I left the forest."

3. Another feral child is John Sesebunya of Uganda. At the age of two, he **ran away** into the jungle, terrified of his father whom he had seen **murder** his mother. He
50 **vaguely** remembers monkeys coming up to him after a few days and offering him roots,° nuts, sweet potatoes and cassava.° The five monkeys were **wary** at first but befriended him within about two weeks and taught him to travel with them, to search for food and to climb
55 trees. John has been studied by **a host of** experts who are convinced he is a **genuine** feral child. When left alone with a group of monkeys, for example, he avoided eye contact and approached them sideways with open palms° in typical simian° fashion. He also tends to greet
60 people with a powerful **hug** in the way that monkeys greet each other. He has, however, learnt to wink,° something monkeys would never do and he has a fine singing voice. John is now a member of the 20-strong Pearl of Africa Children's Choir.
65 (From *Fortean Times The Journal of Strange Phenomena,* # 161, August 2002.)

adopt	= take legal responsibility for a child who is not your own
wood	= small forest
hypersensitivity	= higher degree of sensitivity
root	= the part of the plant that grows into the ground and feeds the plant
cassava	= African root vegetable
palm	= the flat inner part of the hand
simian	= referring to or like a monkey
wink	= close and open an eye quickly

Second reading

C. Answer these questions to get a deeper understanding of the readings.

1. What two facts in section 1 make a strong case for nature having a great influence on our emotional makeup?
2. How can we tell that Klahr is a pretty easygoing guy?
3. To whom is Misha referring when she talks of "my own kind"?
4. Why do you think she did not want to return to the world of her own kind?
5. Why do you think Misha's senses eventually became less heightened?
6. How did scientists test whether John's story was true or not?
7. What habit has John acquired as a result of mixing with humans?
8. Which of his abilities do you think he might have inherited?

Vocabulary in context

D. Find words or phrases in **bold** in the text that mean the same or nearly the same as the words below.

1. untrusting
2. looking for
3. not very clearly
4. small fruit without a pit
5. get along well with
6. make sharper
7. an embrace
8. bring up
9. large numbers of
10. escape from home
11. true or sincere
12. kill someone
13. obtain by researching scientifically
14. join or make friends with
15. not confirmed
16. walk or travel with no specific plan or destination

Discussion

E. With the class, discuss what you find most amazing about these three stories and say which one of these experiences you would prefer to happen to you.

Review and development of relative pronouns: *whose, that, which, who, whom*

Practice

A. PAIR WORK Complete these sentences with *that, which,* or *who/whom.* If there are two possibilities, give them both. Put brackets around the relative pronoun if it can be omitted. Add commas where necessary.

1. People _____ are brought up in loving, caring families are usually quite secure when they grow up.
2. The child _____ they interviewed had been brought up by wolves.
3. Like animals, humans become very good at dealing with environments _____ are challenging and unwelcoming.
4. The silver desert ant is an example of a very small animal _____ has learned to deal with a very hostile environment.
5. IVF _____ has helped many couples overcome the problem of childlessness was initially rejected by many people.
6. The cama _____ scientists in Dubai are studying is a crossbreed between a llama and a camel.
7. Christopher Reeve _____ I have never met has won my admiration for his courage in the face of adversity.
8. Seoul _____ has at least nine bridges is one of the busiest cities in the Far East.

B. Study these statements and answer the questions.

- Which of the statements contain restrictive *(R)* and which contain nonrestrictive *(NR)* relative clauses? How do you recognize them?
- What or whom does the relative pronoun *whose* refer to in each case?
- When can the relative pronoun *whose* be replaced with *of which*?

1. A child whose parents are loving and caring usually develops into a secure adult.
2. Klahr was one of nine children whose parents had given him up for adoption.
3. Misha Defonsecca, whose parents had been murdered by the Nazis, lived with wolves for almost four years of her childhood.
4. I would like to know more about the child whose parents abandoned him in a wood and who was adopted by wolves.
5. The psychologists held a meeting whose purpose was to discuss the importance of genes for the development of personality.
6. John Sesebunya, whose tendency to wink was not learned from monkeys, still remembers how to greet his simian friends.
7. The skills of the Gwich'in, whose village I have visited several times, are a direct response to the challenges of their environment.
8. Silver desert ants are insects whose legs move so quickly that they practically fly over the sand.
9. Hershey, whose street names all relate to chocolate, is a factory town in Pennsylvania.

C. Combine the sentences with *whose.* Make all necessary changes and add commas where appropriate.

EXAMPLE:
> Divorce is common among couples. The couples' parents have also divorced.
> *Divorce is common among couples whose parents have also been divorced.*

1. Twins often have very similar lifestyles. Their upbringings have been completely different.
2. The Masai are a proud African people. Their main source of livelihood is herding sheep and goats.
3. Mozart was a child prodigy by the age of seven. His talents were inherited from his father.
4. I can't remember the name of that bird. Its habitat is a volcano in Colombia.
5. A person is usually a good employee. His or her attitude toward life is positive.
6. Do you know the name of the country? Its capital city is Jakarta.
7. The psychologist is coming to talk to us. You are currently studying his book.
8. The book about the nature-nurture debate is fascinating. I have forgotten its title.

Review and development of relative pronouns: whose, of which

Examples	Rules / Guidelines
Restrictive *Children whose families provide them with a loving, caring environment usually develop into secure adults.*	The relative pronoun *whose* refers to the noun immediately before it. In the restrictive use, it is incorrect to use commas. You can never omit the relative pronoun *whose* at the beginning of the relative clause—whether it is the object or the subject of a sentence.
Nonrestrictive *Betty, whose sons now think she is wonderful, succeeded in her attempt to clear her brother's name.*	The nonrestrictive use differs from the restrictive in that the nonrestrictive clause contains additional information that is not essential to the meaning. Commas are used before and after these clauses.
whose / of which *We went to a lovely village, whose name / the name of which I have completely forgotten.*	Noun + *of which* can take the place of *whose* + noun and is sometimes preferred when the noun is inanimate. Noun + *of which* is more common in British English than in American English.

D. Complete the statements with information about yourself. Then work with a partner and exchange information. Tell the class what you learn about your partner.

1. I like people whose backgrounds _____.
2. I like to read books whose authors _____.
3. I would not go out with / date a person whose clothes _____.
4. I could not be friends with a person whose tastes in music _____.
5. I would never watch a movie whose plot / the plot of which _____.

Test yourself

E. Complete the text with *who, that, which, whom, whose,* or *of which* and add commas if necessary. Indicate with brackets the pronouns that can be omitted.

Betty Anne Waters **(1)** _____ brother was in jail for eighteen years for a crime **(2)** _____ he did not commit believes that if you really want to do something you can do it. Just over twenty years ago, when her brother was wrongly imprisoned for murder, Betty **(3)** _____ was then a high-school dropout mother decided to go back to school and clear her brother's name. The years **(4)** _____ followed this decision were horrendously difficult, not just for Betty but also for her sons **(5)** _____ from a tender age had to get used to having a mom **(6)** _____ could not always do with them the things **(7)** _____ they wanted her to do. In the end, however, Betty, **(8)** _____ qualifications now include degrees in law, economics and teaching, came out on top and thanks to her efforts, her brother was released in March 2000. Betty **(9)** _____ sons are now old enough to appreciate her enormous achievement says that her determination to win was fueled by her anger at a system of justice **(10)** _____ she had discovered was seriously flawed.

Speaking focus

Organizing a presentation

You can organize a presentation effectively by dividing it into three parts: introduction, body, and conclusion. The introduction states your topic and your reasons for talking about it. The body presents facts and information. The conclusion gives a short summary of your presentation. This structure is useful for presentations of all kinds.

A. PAIR WORK What was the happiest day of your life? Take turns telling your stories and asking questions.

B. GROUP WORK Work in groups of four. Carry out a survey of your classmates about some part of their life experience and present the results to the rest of the class. First choose a general topic—education, travel, work, relationships, accidents, or another you are interested in. Then plan two survey questions on your topic. Below are kinds of questions you can use.

> Have you ever …? What was the first …? How often do you …?
> What was the best / worst / happiest / most difficult …? How many …?

C. Form new groups with students who prepared different survey questions. Take turns asking and answering your survey questions. Be sure to write down all the answers you receive.

D. CLASS TASK Go back to your original group. Put together the answers you received and work together to prepare a short presentation in three parts: an introduction, the answers to each of your questions, and a conclusion. Then take turns giving your presentations to the class. Each group member should present one part.

Many web sites conduct online surveys that ask people about their experiences and opinions. At one web site, 27.2% of the people who answered said they had been stuck inside an elevator, 11.1% said they had experienced an earthquake, 5.3% said they had met a U.S. president, and 10.7% said they had had their car stolen.

[source: http://www.howstuffworks.com/survey-archive.htm]

A. Discuss what you understand by the words *entrepreneur* and *personnel manager*. What is the difference between the two? Brainstorm and list all the adjectives and expressions you know that you think might apply to the personality of each.

EXAMPLE:

entrepreneur	***career manager***
creative thinker	*very obedient*
workaholic	*not very adventurous*

With the class, make a complete list on the board of all the words and expressions class members listed.

B. Read the text to try and understand the words or expressions in **bold**.

What **drives** entrepreneurs and career managers in their **relentless quest** for professional and financial success? It may surprise you to know that both entrepreneurs and career managers share a common problem: they may both have suffered **maltreatment** at the hands of their parents in childhood and in particular, at the hands of their fathers. There, however, the similarity stops, as the two have very different ways of dealing with their problem fathers. Children who have selfish, uncaring fathers with **enormous egos** but few achievements spend most of their time trying **in vain** to make their fathers proud of them. This leaves them feeling insecure and **inadequate.** As a result, they have a strong desire to please **authority.** They seek the emotional security they never had as children by establishing good, trusting relationships with senior managers, who take the place of their **negligent** or **abusive** fathers and who foster their careers. Although they are **innovative,** they try to avoid reliving the adversity of their childhood by taking only highly calculated risks.

In contrast, entrepreneurs set out to prove that they can **flout** authority, that they are no longer the victims of aggressive, **repressive** parents. They love to **go it alone** and find it impossible to **kowtow** to any authority figure. They not only take enormous risks, they actually **get a buzz out of** professional risk-taking. They are not only innovative; they **think the unthinkable** and they simply love to challenge the **status quo.** These differences are due not just to the different forms of abuse the entrepreneurs and career managers receive from their parents. They can also be **accounted for** in social origins. Whereas entrepreneurs often come from poor, working, or immigrant families, career mangers tend to come from more **privileged** sectors of society.

C. PAIR WORK Find a word or expression in this list that has the same or a similar meaning to the words or expressions in **bold** in the text.

1. high opinion of oneself _____
2. insulting _____
3. careless in doing their duty ____
4. the way things are now _____
5. obey without questioning _____
6. never-ending _____
7. motivates _____
8. survive without help _____
9. incompetent ____
10. enjoy enormously _____
11. be extremely creative _____
12. with cultural and economic advantages _____
13. explain with reference to _____
14. cruelty _____
15. unreasonably strict ____
16. ignore with great pleasure _____
17. without success _____
18. people in control ____
19. having new ideas _____

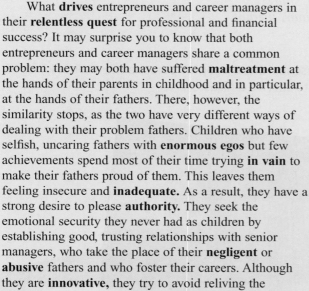

D. GROUP WORK Use the new words and expressions in **bold** in exercise B to talk about someone in your country or community who has been highly successful despite or because of adversity in childhood.

Listening strategy

Guessing vocabulary

When you hear an unfamiliar word, don't stop—keep listening. If the word is important, it will probably be repeated, and you will be able to guess what it means from the context in which you hear it.

Before you listen

A. You are going to listen to a radio show about people who have lived through natural disasters. What disasters have happened in your country? What kinds of disasters happen in other countries? Have you ever experienced a natural disaster?

First listening

B. Listen and take notes about the disaster—what the people did during the disaster and what they did afterwards.

Second listening

C. Listen again and try to work out the meaning of the words below. Take notes to help you. Then with a partner, discuss the meaning of the words.

Carol's story: *torrential, sludge*
David's story: *unconscious, therapy*

After listening

D. How would you describe these people's personalities? What kinds of people are most likely to survive a disaster?

Test yourself

E. Listen to this talk about another disaster and answer the questions.

What does *severe* mean?
a. extremely hot   **b.** broken in pieces   **c.** very bad   **d.** large number

What does *incredible* mean?
a. difficult to believe   **b.** very dangerous   **c.** rare and expensive   **d.** too many to count

Writing a concluding paragraph

Before you write

A. GROUP WORK Discuss what you understand by the nature-nurture debate. Give examples from your own life or family of how you think one or the other has influenced you or a member of your family. Then reorder each of the sets of scrambled sentences into coherent paragraphs. Identify which is the introductory paragraph and in which order the other two paragraphs should follow it.

Paragraph A

1. Let us suppose, for example, that your genotype predisposes you to being very tall, but the diet in your environment is extremely poor.
2. Although every organism has a unique genetic code called the genotype, this alone does not determine exactly how a creature will be physically.
3. The environment has a big influence on the genotype, and the results of this influence are expressed in the phenotype.
4. In contrast to the position mentioned above, the influence can work in the other direction, i.e., the environment can influence genes just as genes can dictate the choice of environment.
5. You may not grow nearly as tall as a relative with a similar genotype and a good diet.

Paragraph B

1. When a newborn baby has people nearby, for example, it responds favorably with lower heart and respiration rates.
2. Once firmly established within the social group, the groups themselves provide us with the environment that helps us learn to become successful human beings.
3. Humans are social creatures, so we seek other humans because we would be lonely and depressed without them.
4. We are, therefore, naturally driven to live in social groups.
5. A creature's genes will, in general, motivate it to seek environments that will help it survive and avoid those that could be hostile to it.

Paragraph C

1. Here we seek to demonstrate that seeing the nature-nurture debate in such black-and-white terms is a mistake.
2. Often, however, the answer is not so straightforward.
3. We often see or hear the question, "Is this due to genes or is it due to the environment?"
4. Genes and environment influence each other greatly, and their effects can almost never be disentangled.
5. Sometimes there is a straightforward answer— in the case, for example, of hereditary diseases such as Parkinson's disease or color blindness.
6. Is Enrique a brilliant guitarist because his father was too or is he a brilliant guitarist because he has been able to practice the guitar from an early age?

B. In the same groups, read the rearranged text and underline the correct option.

1. This text is most likely:
   a. a newspaper article
   b. a business letter
   c. an academic essay
   d. an advertise-ment
   e. a company report

2. The text mainly:
   a. describes something in detail
   b. narrates a sequence of events
   c. explains what something is or how it works
   d. discusses an important issue
   e. argues a case for one position

Write

C. Write out the rearranged text and write a concluding paragraph, i.e., a fourth paragraph that summarizes the main points of the text. Then join another group and read and discuss your concluding paragraphs. With the class, discuss the main "ingredients" of a concluding paragraph.

A. GROUP WORK Work in groups and write a ten-item quiz about people, places, and animals. All the clues should contain the possessive relative pronoun *whose*. Join another group and take turns asking your questions. Then choose the most interesting five items from both of your quizzes and use these to test the rest of the class.

> EXAMPLE: *It's a person whose work is to sing and entertain. (a singer)*

B. Work alone. Imagine you are going to find a roommate. Here are some notes about different people who have offered to be your roommate. Read the notes, decide which of the people you would or would not accept as a roommate, and write your reasons. Then find a partner and listen to his or her decisions. Discuss which were different from yours and why.

> EXAMPLE: *I wouldn't have a roommate whose job is insecure. She might lose her job and not have enough money to pay her share of the rent.*

1. job is insecure
2. has a very luxurious lifestyle
3. has a fun-loving but sensible attitude toward life
4. schedule can mean he or she has to work nights
5. references from his or her bank manager are very good
6. girlfriend or boyfriend seems very possessive
7. taste in music is mostly classical and jazz
8. taste in food is mostly fast food and canned food
9. appearance is neat and tidy
10. has a very loud voice
11. family lives in another state and clearly cares about him or her a lot
12. outside interests include soccer, dancing, and going to museums

C. CLASS TASK Organize a debate on the topic below.

An employer should have the right to see a report of a future employee's genotype.

For more detail about Upbringing, view the CNN video. Activities to accompany the video begin on page 144.

Learning

Communication

Discussing the effects of education

Describing the qualities of a good teacher

Structuring information logically in oral presentations

Grammar

Review of future forms and uses

Future progressive, future perfect, and future perfect progressive

Vocabulary

Education

Learning styles

Skills

Scanning a newspaper article: education

Listening and using number cues for note taking

Writing a formal letter

1 Warm Up

A. PAIR WORK Describe what you see in the pictures.

- Where do you think the people are?
- What do you think they are doing?
- Are there any illiterate people in your country? If so, where could they learn to read and write?

B. Match the definitions below with one of the words in the box.

> forebear   trader   pastoralist   elder   settler   educator   shepherd   herder

1. person who takes an interest in helping people to learn _____
2. person who is one of the oldest members of his or her social group _____
3. person who helps move animals from one place to another _____
4. person who buys and sells things _____
5. person who moves to and stays in a developing area _____
6. person who takes care of sheep and goats _____
7. person who makes a living from keeping sheep and goats _____
8. member of your family who lived a long time before you _____

C. PAIR WORK Where did your family come from originally? What kind of education did they have? What kind of work did they do? Tell the class what you learned about your partner.

Paying attention to pronouns

To avoid repeating nouns or noun phrases and for the sake of clarity, a writer often refers back to something already mentioned with the use of a pronoun. Look out for pronouns and note what they are referring to. This will help you to understand the text.

Before you read

A. GROUP WORK Talk about the people you see in these pictures. Which continent do you think they come from? Why? What do you think their jobs are? Why? What kind of education do you think they have received?

First reading

B. Scan the reading and determine whether the statements are True *(T)* or False *(F)*. Correct the false statements and underline the information in the text that supports the true ones.

1. Thirty-five percent of the Masai are illiterate. _____
2. The Masai customs and lifestyle have not changed much over the centuries. _____
3. The Masai lost 10% of their land when they signed a treaty with the British. _____
4. The work of the young educators with the shepherds is easy. _____
5. So far, 1,800 young herders have learned to read and write thanks to the young educators. _____
6. The literacy classes take place in modern school buildings. _____
7. Children who go to school work as shepherds in the afternoons so that their brothers and sisters can attend literacy classes. _____
8. In addition to reading and writing, the young Masai educators strongly believe in teaching Masai culture to the shepherds. _____

Shepherd School

Johnson Kinyago, a sun-dried Masai herder, has two sons. "One is **a genius**—he can identify every animal and find water anywhere. So he's with the goats," he says proudly. "The other is stupid so he's in school." At a
5 cattle market in Laikipia in northern Kenya, other Masai elders nod° their **approval.** Herding is for bright sparks,° school for "thickies," all of them say. Only 35% of Masai children attend school. The reason is that pastoralists depend on their children's labor, so even if persuaded of
10 the **merits** of school, few could spare° their ablest **offspring.** The result is an illiteracy rate of over 90%, leaving the Masai **vulnerable to** abuse° from their more worldly neighbors.

  With their stretched ear lobes, their ochre-stained
15 warriors, and gap-toothed brides, the Masai live much as they have for centuries, but in a world which has changed **radically.** When their—illiterate—forebears made peace with the first British settlers, they unwittingly° signed away 90% of their land. The
20 remaining arid **patch** no longer supports their swollen° population. During a recent three-year drought, more than 89% of their animals died; and the proud Masai are now humiliatingly dependent on food aid.

25   In an effort to break this **debilitating** cycle, a group of educated young Masai have established nonformal classes across Laikipia's rocky hills,
30 bringing school to the shepherds. These young educators understand the prejudices° they are **confronting.** "My father hated me so he chased me off to school," says Peter Lowara, a social worker with the
35 group, which calls itself Osiligi, or Hope, in Masai. "It was terrible—I felt like I had no **prospects.**" But they also know the consequences of resisting change.

  "Land **issues** have caused a crisis in pastoralism, and this is threatening our whole people," says James
40 Legei, Osiligi's program officer. "Unless we find alternatives, we will die; which means we must become educated."

  Over the past four years, meeting under shady° trees or in sheltered **hollows,** 1,800 young herders have
45 acquired basic literacy, Swahili, English, and math. Nearly 100 have continued into the formal education system and the prospect of jobs, while those remaining with their herds should at least now be able to read the

instructions on packets of veterinary drugs in English, or
50 hold their own against Swahili-speaking livestock°
traders for a fair price.

Fixing his blackboard to a tree, Joseph Saoi proudly
shows off his class of a dozen bright shepherds, aged
five to thirteen. Arranged along another fallen tree, eyes
55 rapt to the board and hands clutching dog-eared exercise
books, they **radiate** enthusiasm for learning. Most see
duller **siblings** troop off to school every morning,
leaving them behind. But for these two hours of the late
afternoon—timed so the regular schoolchildren can take
60 over herding after class—they have a chance to catch up.

According to Osiligi, the devastating effects of the
drought caused some Masai to rethink their traditional
disregard for schooling. But at the same time it
crippled° their ability to pay the fees. This leaves girls,
65 whom the Masai consider a poor investment because
they will be married outside the family, further from
school than ever. "I see more and more girls at my
classes, because they are the lowest **priority** for formal
education," says Saoi.
70 The freedom to adapt its classes is one of Osiligi's
strengths. Besides reading, writing, and math, students are
taught the basics of animal **husbandry,** hygiene,° and
Masai culture. According to the national curriculum, they

would instead be forced to study crops such as coffee
and pyrethrum, which do not grow in Laikipia's arid
75 soil. "The education system in Kenya is killing
individual cultures," says (James) Legei. "It has to be
more sensitive to the particular needs of each
community. If you educate my way of life out of me and
there is no job at the end of it, what then? Education
80 kills some traditions," he continues. "But the thing is to
control the **pace** of change, so you retain others, together
with a sense of identity, which is crucial."°

["Shepherd School" by James Astill. *The Guardian
Education Supplement,* 2 April, 2002.]

---

nod = move head up and down in agreement
bright spark = very intelligent person
spare = do without
abuse = unfair or bad treatment
unwittingly = unintentionally
swollen = greatly increased
prejudice = unfair dislike of something or somebody
shady = protecting from sunlight
livestock = farm animals
cripple = limit greatly
hygiene = science of personal health, especially cleanliness
crucial = extremely important

Vocabulary in context

C. Find words or phrases in **bold** in the text with
the same or similar meanings to the words or
phrases in the list.

1. farming _____
2. low opinion of _____
3. extraordinarily intelligent person _____
4. piece of land _____
5. speed of an activity _____
6. brothers and sisters _____
7. benefits _____
8. important factor _____
9. children _____
10. experience or face _____
11. produce or send out _____
12. very low part in the ground _____
13. matters _____
14. professional future _____
15. weakening _____
16. enormously, greatly _____
17. exposed to _____
18. agreement _____

D. GROUP WORK After reading the text again
for a detailed understanding, write outline notes in
which you cover these eight points.

1. what traditional Masai pastoralists think of
   formal education

2. the reasons the British were able to persuade
   the Masai to sign a contract that was not very
   favorable to them

3. the reason food aid is humiliating for the
   Masai

4. the reasons some young educators want to
   provide education to all Masai children,
   including the shepherd children

5. the reason the Masai's opinion of formal
   schooling is beginning to change

6. the reason the Masai are unwilling to pay for
   formal education for their daughters

7. two disadvantages of formal education for
   communities like the Masai

Discussion

E. Discuss any customs that have disappeared in
your country as a result of formal education. Would
you like these customs to be reintroduced? Give
reasons for your opinion.

Review of future forms and uses

Future progressive, future perfect, and future perfect progressive

Practice

A. PAIR WORK Read the uses listed below and match each use with one of the statements.

EXAMPLE: *make a prediction (passive voice)* _b_

1. talk about a meeting or personal arrangement (active voice) _____
2. make a prediction (active voice) _____
3. make a prediction (passive voice) _____
4. talk about the future result of a present cause (active voice) _____
5. talk about a future result of a future cause (passive voice) _____
6. talk about the future result of a present action (active voice) _____
7. talk about a scheduled future action (active voice) _____
8. make a decision at the moment of speaking (active voice) _____

a. We **arrive** at the Masai region at noon.
b. You **are going to be saddened** by what you see.
c. I'll **do my best** to explain why this is the case.
d. Unfortunately, there has been a drought this year, and the Masai livestock **are going to die.**
e. The Masai **will have to find** other sources of income.
f. With their literacy programs, the young Masai educators **are going to try** to save their community from extinction.
g. The educators **are meeting** with UNESCO officials next week to try and get more support for their programs.
h. The Masai girls **won't be married** within their own extended family.

B. GROUP WORK Compare your answers in exercise A. Then read statements a to h again and decide what is the grammatical form of the verbs in **bold.**

EXAMPLE: *a. We **arrive** at the Masai region at noon.* (simple future tense active voice)

C. Imagine you have made an arrangement to meet an old friend. Complete the statements below. Share your information with a partner and tell the class what you learn about his or her arrangement.

1. I'm meeting an old friend on _____.
2. We are going to have coffee in _____.
3. I haven't seen him / her for a long time, so it's going to be _____.
4. He / She will be surprised because I _____.
5. We will probably talk for _____.
6. We will have to be quick though as the coffee shop closes at _____.

D. PAIR WORK Read the statements and decide on the answers to these questions. Which are in the future progressive form (active voice)? Which are in the future perfect (active voice)? Which are in the future perfect (passive voice)? Which are in the future perfect progressive (active voice)?

1. In two or three years' time, the life of the Masai *will have changed* a lot.
2. By the end of this decade, most of them *will have been working* for several years in very different occupations from the ones they have today.
3. All their livestock *will have been sold.*
4. Most of the Masai *will have learned* to read and write.
5. Some *will be working* in offices; others, in shops.
6. Thanks to the young educators, not all of the Masai customs *will have been forgotten,* however.
7. By 2010, these young educators *will have been running* their literacy programs for almost a decade.
8. They *will have succeeded* in preserving many of the Masai customs through these programs.

Future progressive, future perfect, and future perfect progressive

Form	Example	Use	Meaning
Future progressive: *will* + *be* + present participle	*Very soon we will all be living in unpolluted environments.*	future events that will last for a period of time	in progress at a certain time in the future
Future perfect: *will* + *have* + past participle	*We will have abandoned the consumer society by the middle of this century.*	before a certain time in the future	future events happening before other future events
Future perfect progressive: *will* + *have* + *been* + present participle	*By the end of the decade, we will have been using videophones for several years.*	up until a certain point in the future	continuous and/or repeated actions continuing into the future

E. GROUP WORK Use the structures in exercise D to make statements about the topics below.

> EXAMPLE: *1. By the end of the decade, scientists will have found efficient alternatives to fossil fuels.*

1. by the end of the decade: scientists / fossil fuels / find
2. in a few years' time: the problem of paralysis / solve
3. very soon: many of us / video telephones / use
4. in about twenty years' time: the hole in the ozone layer / disappear
5. by the end of the decade: it is unlikely that / human cloning / permit
6. very soon: we / hydrogen-fueled cars / drive
7. maybe, by the end of the decade: problems with the international stock markets / simpler lifestyles / lead to
8. before the end of the decade: all of us / GM (genetically modified) foods / eat / several years

Test yourself

F. Choose an appropriate future form from any of those in this Grammar in Detail to complete the dialog.

S1: I **(1)** _____ (leave) for Canada next week.

S2: Oh? What **(2)** _____ (do) there?

S1: Research. Do you think you **(3)** _____ (be able to) come and visit me?

S2: I **(4)** _____ certainly (try). By the way, I have a brother in Canada.

S1: Is that so? I **(5)** _____ (have to) look him up.

S2: Yeah, I **(6)** _____ (give) you his contact details tomorrow.

S1: How long has he been living there?

S2: Well, I'd say that by the end of this year, he **(7)** _____ (live) there for five years.

S1: That's a long time. I guess he **(8)** _____ (get to know) a lot of people by now.

S2: Sure thing. But he **(9)** _____ (look for) a change of country soon. He doesn't like to stay in one place for more than five years.

S1: Gee, I hope he **(10)** _____ (left) by the time I get there!

S2: No way. I'd know about it if he had plans for leaving that soon.

Speaking focus

Structuring information in a presentation

In the body or central part of a presentation, you can structure your information by stating a main idea and then giving supporting details to explain your idea, just as you do when writing.

A. PAIR WORK In pairs, discuss these questions. Who have been your best teachers? What are some things they did that made them good teachers?

B. GROUP WORK Prepare a two- to three-minute presentation on the characteristics of a good teacher. Choose three characteristics that you think are important—for example, patience. Then think of examples and explanations for each characteristic. Organize your ideas into a presentation. All group members should take notes and prepare to give the presentation.

C. GROUP WORK Join with students from other groups. Take turns standing up and each giving your presentation to this new group. Take notes on the other speakers' ideas.

D. CLASS TASK Discuss these questions.

- Were each group's ideas similar or different?
- Were there any characteristics that everyone agreed on?
- What should future teachers learn in their training courses?

Today, there are about 140 million children in the world ages six to eleven who do not go to school—about one in five. An additional $7 billion per year would be enough to provide schools for all these children. To put this need in a different perspective, people in Europe spend $11 billion per year on ice cream.

5 Vocabulary in Detail

A. Read the text to understand the words or expressions in **bold.** What do you think each word or expression means?

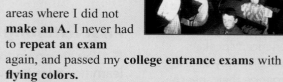

For a long time, my high school days were not the happiest days of my life. I was an **undisciplined** student and **goofed off** a lot in classes. Basically, I did not find the lessons very **motivating,** so it was hard for me to **concentrate. I got into** a lot of **trouble** and was often **punished.** Punishment usually meant I was not allowed to go to Phys. Ed. and sports was my favorite class. I used to **cut** classes a lot, so I often **failed** tests and exams. Then a new **principal** came to our school. She **encouraged** teachers to experiment with more challenging teaching methods by getting the kids to **participate** more in class. As a result, I changed completely—from being an **unruly,** uncooperative student to being a **highly focused,** enthusiastic learner. I soon **caught up** and started to **get A grades** in most subjects and worked incredibly hard to **improve in** those areas where I did not **make an A.** I never had to **repeat an exam** again, and passed my **college entrance exams** with **flying colors.**

The **going got tough** again at college, as higher education is not free in this country. The **fees** at my college were quite high, and my parents are not wealthy, so I had to **work my way** through my first degree. I worked **part time** as a waiter in a local restaurant. Graduate school was much easier in financial terms. I got a summa cum laude in my first degree, so I was **awarded** scholarships for my graduate courses. Now I have a well-paid job and I'm very happy. I shall always be very grateful to that **inspiring** high school director who changed my life.

B. PAIR WORK Compare your answers to exercise A with a partner. Then complete the statements with one of the expressions in **bold** or with a derivation of one of these expressions.

EXAMPLE:

I was a very _____ high school student. I never goofed off.
I was a very disciplined high school student. I never goofed off.

1. Some of my friends, on the other hand, were not very _____ and they cut classes a lot.

2. They were often _____ for their lack of discipline at school.

3. When we got a new and very _____ English teacher, everything changed and my friends became _____ students who never again _____ a test or an exam.

4. Like me, all of them were _____ _____, which helped pay for the very high _____ when we first went to _____.

C. Match the expressions on the left with their meanings on the right.

1. the going gets tough   **a.** get really good grades

2. drop out of a course or program   **b.** things become very difficult

3. pass with flying colors   **c.** reach the same level as others

4. make a mess of (a test or an essay)   **d.** not progress at the same rate as others

5. catch up with (course content)   **e.** leave or stop taking part in

6. get left behind   **f.** do something very badly

D. PAIR WORK Talk about important aspects of your own experience of education—at grade school, high school, or college. Use vocabulary from above. Then share with the class what you learned about your partner.

Listening and using number cues for note taking

Experienced speakers usually give very clear cues to organize their speech. These cues are often numbers.

EXAMPLE: *There are four types of…*

You can use number cues to help organize the notes you are taking as you listen and to check that you have noted all the important points.

Before you listen

A. PAIR WORK Discuss these questions with a partner. How do you like to learn about a new subject—by reading about it, hearing about it, seeing it on TV, or by doing a project? Do you think this is the same for everybody?

First listening

B. You are going to hear a radio talk about learning styles. You will hear about three different types of learners: auditory, visual, and kinesthetic. Listen and take notes to help you decide which type corresponds most to you. Then, in groups, discuss which type you are. Give your reasons.

Second listening

C. Listen again and take notes about ways that learners of your type can learn languages.

After listening

D. Check how many students in the class there are for each type of learning style. What activities could people with different styles use to learn other things—for example, playing a new sport?

Test yourself

E. Listen to a talk about how to be more creative and take notes. Then answer the questions.

1. What is the speaker's main idea?
   a. Some people are more creative than others.
   b. Art is the best way to develop creativity.
   c. Creativity is connected with travel.
   d. All people can increase their creativity.

2. According to the speaker, why does art enhance creativity?
   a. It is stimulating for your mind.
   b. It takes you away from daily life.
   c. It shows you many new sights.
   d. You don't have to do it well.

Writing a formal letter

Before you write

A. GROUP WORK Discuss the meaning of these words and expressions and use them to talk about the system of education in your country.

student loan	transcript	final exams
undergraduate program	coursework	thesis
graduate degree	continuous assessment	dissertation
vocational training	summer school	academic essay or
lectures	résumé	assignment

> **FYI**
>
> *Graduate degree, graduate student* and *graduate studies* are called *postgraduate degree, postgraduate student,* and *postgraduate studies* in British English

B. Read these paragraphs below taken from the body of a letter and arrange them in a logical sequence: introductory, supporting, and concluding paragraphs. Then write the reorganized letter. Make sure it looks like a real letter.

- Where will you put your address?
- Where will you put the date?
- Where will you put the name and address of the addressee?
- How will you start and finish the letter?

Write

C. GROUP WORK Write a formal letter of at least three paragraphs (introductory, supporting, concluding) for one of these situations.

1. You are a graduate student at an English-speaking university and you have run into financial difficulties and fear you might not be able to complete the course. Write to your student counselor to ask for suggestions about how you could earn a little extra money so that you can complete your course.

2. You are currently working in your own country but wish to pursue graduate studies in an English-speaking country. Write to the dean of the Department for Overseas Students, giving the necessary information about yourself and requesting his or her advice.

> You will see from my résumé that I have had previous teaching experience, so I am confident that I will be able to combine my graduate studies with my duties as a teaching assistant. In addition, the subject I would have to teach was my undergraduate major, for which I was awarded a summa cum laude, so class preparation should not be too difficult.
>
> You will find my transcript attached to my résumé, together with a reference from my last teaching post. I would be pleased to provide you with any further information you may require. In the meantime, I look forward to hearing from you.
>
> I wish to apply for one of the teaching assistantships which your department advertised in this week's issue of *The Campus Educator,* and to this end I enclose my résumé.
>
> I am motivated to apply for this post because, over the past few months, there has been a serious economic crisis in my country. As a result, the monthly scholarship I receive is no longer enough for me to survive on. It would be most distressing to have to drop out of my course at this stage as I am enjoying it very much. If I can count on a small additional income, such as a teaching assistantship, then I will be able to complete my course of study.

D. Exchange letters with a group that chose a different situation from yours. Read their letter and write a reply. Then read the reply you received to your letter and discuss it.

A. PAIR WORK Find a partner who is someone in the class you know well. First work alone and write brief notes about how you imagine your partner's life will be ten years from now. Use the following questions to guide your thinking but use your imagination too.

- Where will that person be living?
- What job will he or she be doing?
- What personal changes will have taken place in his or her life? (marital status, children, etc.)
- What professional changes will have taken place? (degrees, other qualifications)
- What kind of travel experiences will he or she have had?

Then work with your partner and use your notes to say how you imagine his or her life will be ten years from now. After you have listened, discuss what you heard. Do you agree or disagree? Give your reasons.

B. PAIR WORK You are going to describe the qualities of a teacher. With the class, decide whether you are going to describe a grade school teacher, a high school teacher, or a college professor. Brainstorm for all the qualities you would expect to find in this person. Work in groups and choose the six most important qualities. Number them from one to six, with number one being the most important. Share your decisions with the whole class; try to reach an agreement about the six most important qualities and their order of importance

C. CLASS TASK Organize a debate on the topic below.

All college fees should be abolished. The state should offer free college education to all students who want it.

For more detail about Learning, view the CNN video. Activities to accompany the video begin on page 145.

Ruth Handler, creator of the *Barbie* doll.

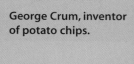
George Crum, inventor of potato chips.

George Washington Carver, agricultural researcher.

Achievement

Communication

Predicting what might have happened after twenty years

Discussing the merits of certain advances in science and technology

Using convincing reasons in oral presentations

Grammar

Review of modal verbs (active voice)

Modal verbs (passive voice)

Vocabulary

Professional achievement

Uses of *job*, *work*, and *career*

Understanding proverbs

Skills

Scanning scientific texts

Listening for examples

Writing an academic essay

1 Warm Up

A. PAIR WORK Look at the pictures. Say who the people are and why they became famous.

B. Match the things on the left with the people responsible for them on the right. Use verbs like *write, invent, create,* and *research* to talk about the inventors or researchers.

EXAMPLE: *The Sony Corporation was created by Akio Morita. He was from Japan.*

1. Microsoft software
2. aluminum foil
3. animal cloning
4. *One Hundred Years of Solitude*
5. the Sony Corporation
6. jeans
7. the Web

a. Keith Campbell and Ian Wilnut (Scotland)
b. Tim Berners-Lee (England)
c. Gabriel Garcia Marquez (Colombia)
d. Bill Gates (U.S.)
e. Richard S. Reynolds (U.S.)
f. Levi Strauss (U.S.)
g. Akio Morita (Japan)

C. Complete the table.

Verb	Noun (thing)	Noun (person / agent)	Adjective
1. invent	_____	_____	inventive
2. _____	_____		congested
3. _____	_____	developer	_____ AND developing
4. achieve	_____	_____	_____
5. innovate	_____	innovator	_____
6. accomplish	accomplishment		_____
7.	commerce		_____

Reading strategy

Thinking ahead

As soon as you see the title of a reading, study it and look at the first few lines. Then begin to ask yourself logical questions about the reading. As you read, try to provide answers to the questions you pose for yourself. Remember, reading is always an active process.

Before you read

A. GROUP WORK Speculate about how old you think each person in the pictures is, where he or she comes from, and which of the jobs each person does: computer software expert, company director, mechanical engineer, genetic and chemical engineer.

First reading

B. Scan the personal profiles below. Decide who the people in the pictures are and confirm their age, profession, focus of research (transportation, energy, software, hardware, Internet, medicine) and their country of residence.

Mar Hershenson

Ethan Zucherman

Joseph Cargnelli

Suzie Hwang Pun

Young Achievers

Suzie Hwang Pun Think of Suzie Hwang Pun as a traffic cop° for genes. The 27-year-old chemical engineer uses polymers to carry injected genes through the bloodstream. With a system of molecular **tags,** she
5 can direct a gene, for instance, one that blocks cancer progression, to just the right spot—like the **nuclei** of cells in a tumor.° It is a trick that could solve a problem in gene therapy research: a new gene does no good if it does not reach the right place. While viruses are the
10 typical delivery vehicles in gene therapy, they are hard to manufacture and can be **intercepted** by the immune system. Pun's polymer materials avoid those problems and open the possibility of delivering drugs, as well as genes, with **exquisite precision.** "This is the tip of the
15 iceberg,"° says Caltech chemical engineer Mark Davis. He was so excited by Pun's accomplishments as a graduate student in his lab that he founded Insert Therapeutics in Pasadena, Calif., primarily to commercialize her work. Pun **jumped at the chance** to
20 be a senior scientist and employee number one. If all goes well, her technology could enter **human trials** within a few years.

    Joseph Cargnelli Hydrogen fuel cells promise to **break the** world's fossil fuel **habit** without a puff° of
25 carbon dioxide, thanks to the efforts of Joseph Cargnelli. In 1995, in a small room above his family's machine

shop in Toronto, Canada, the mechanical engineer and two associates launched Hydrogenics. The company **made its mark** producing test stations that Cargnelli
30 designed to put fuel cells through their paces.° The test units accelerated the work of fuel cell developers and secured Hydrogenics' $84 million initial public offering in 2000. Today, Cargnelli, now thirty-two and vice president, is worth millions. But the roar of
35 equipment still fills his shop-floor office at a complex on Toronto's west side, where Hydrogenics is developing its own fuel cell engines. Last year, in a six-month span, Cargnelli's team prototyped° a fuel cell generator and transformed it into a backup power
40 supply to keep cell tower antennas and their networks alive during blackouts.° To Cargnelli, success just means one more step toward the hydrogen economy.

    Mar Hershenson Hershenson came to Silicon Valley from Barcelona, Spain, for a summer job, met
45 her future husband, and stayed, bringing a bit of her native city to California in the form of Barcelona Design, which she co-founded in 1999. The company produces software and intellectual property, designed by the 30-year-old Hershenson, for quickly optimizing°
50 the design of analog circuits for cell phones, TVs, and DVD players. Previously, engineers could spend a year designing a single analog chip. With the solution of Barcelona Design, **custom** analog circuits can be finished in hours. Hershenson's **breakthrough** was to

represent circuits with equations that can be solved
mathematically. She learned the technique in a course
taught by Stephen Boyd, the Stanford professor with
whom she launched the company. The firm, which has
forty-five employees, has raised $44 million and lined up
60 several large clients, including the chip-making giant
STMicroelectronics. **Bursting with** ideas, Hershenson
plans to apply the Barcelona Design technology to a
wider range of circuitry.

    Ethan Zuckerman When Ethan Zuckerman went to
65 Ghana in 1993 as a Fulbright scholar, he immediately tried
to get online; he was a Usenet junkie and **eager to** e-mail
his girlfriend (now his wife). But in **bustling** Accra, he
found only one temperamental° net connection.
Subsequently, Zuckerman, who is now twenty-eight,
70 became vice president of a famous dot-com company and
was soon a millionaire, but he never forgot Ghana's
inadequate communications. In July 1999, he left the dot-
com company and in February 2000 co-founded
Geekcorps in North Adams, Mass. Geekcorps sends

75 **volunteers** with information technology **expertise** to
developing countries for four-month stints, where they
help businesses—from furniture factories to radio
stations—get online, expand sales, and thus create jobs.
One volunteer even helped launch the Ghanaian
80 parliament's web sites. Funded by foundations, aid
agencies, and private donors, Geekcorps has sent thirty-
five tutors to Ghana and several other countries. And
there is no **shortage** of volunteers: more than 1,100
people are on Geekcorps's waiting list.

---

cop = informal word for police officer
tumor = a growth of diseased tissue
tip of the iceberg = the small beginnings of something much larger
puff = very small amount of wind
put through…paces = try out, test
prototype = the first model of something produced
blackout = failure of electricity
optimize = use fully
temperamental = not very reliable, unpredictable

Second reading

C. PAIR WORK Read the text again and
complete the outline notes. In some cases, you will
have to supply the headings, and in others, the
details.

1. two major disadvantages of using viruses as
   vehicles in gene therapy
   a. _____
   b. _____

2. Hwang Pun's solution for directing genes _____
   _____

3. two of Joseph Cargnelli's achievements so far
   a. _____
   b. _____

4. ____ make a major contribution to the
   hydrogen economy

5. ____ _____
   a. has set up a software company called
   Barcelona Design
   b. _____

6. Mar Hershenson's ambition _____

7. problem Ethan Zuckerman experienced in
   Ghana _____

8. Ethan's solution to Ghana's problem _____

Vocabulary in context

D. Find a word or expression in **bold** in the text
with the same or a similar meaning to the words
and expressions below.

1. very full of
2. inadequate
   amount of
3. become famous
4. supreme accuracy
5. specialized
   knowledge
6. discovery
7. enthusiastic about
8. tests on people
9. prevent from
   continuing on
   a journey

10. centers
11. people who work
    for no or small
    amounts of money
12. stop doing
    something you have
    done for ages
13. full of activity
14. made to suit a
    specific purpose
15. accept an
    opportunity with
    great enthusiasm
16. labels

Discussion

E. With the class, discuss the young achievers in
the text. Which one is the most philanthropic?
Which one is the most ambitious? Who might
have problems with the ethical aspect of his or
her research? Who would or wouldn't you like to
be? Give your reasons.

Review of modal verbs (active voice)

Modal verbs (passive voice)

Practice

A. PAIR WORK Match the modal verbs in **bold** with the descriptions in the box. One description can be applied to two of the sentences.

were obliged or forced to
used to
it is possible but it hasn't happened yet
there is little doubt that
do not need or have an obligation to
is able to
feel a strong personal need or obligation to

1. She **can** direct a gene to the right spot. _____
2. It is a trick that **could** solve a problem in gene therapy research. _____
3. Previously, engineers **could** spend a year designing a single analog chip. ____
4. In Kenya, the intelligent children of Masai pastoralists **do not have to** attend school. ____
5. Some young Masai educators feel that they **must** teach all children to read and write. ___
6. They believe that educated people **may** be able to look after themselves better. _____
7. Masai who **had to** look after livestock when they were children instead of going to school now find it impossible to find any other kind of job. _____
8. They **must** be very unhappy when they think about their future prospects. _____

B. Match each modal perfect verb in **bold** with the correct use or function.

a. to mention one possibility among several with reference to a past action
b. to express irritation or criticism of an action not taken
c. to express a strong supposition (near certainty) about a past action
d. to express regret about an action not taken
e. to express uncertainty about an action taken
f. to express disbelief about something that was supposed to have happened
g. to express an expectation about a past event
h. to express regret about a past action that was taken

1. He **must have** lived a long time in an Arab country. _____
2. We **should have** studied harder for the test. ____
3. I **might have** left my umbrella on the bus. _____
4. They **could have** phoned to cancel the appointment. _____
5. Jennifer **can't have** said those horrible things about me. _____
6. David **should have** arrived by now. _____
7. She **could have** chosen that job because of the travel opportunities. _____
8. I **shouldn't have** stayed up so late tonight. _____

C. GROUP WORK Study the passive constructions in **bold** in the sentences below. Then formulate a rule for the passive of modal verbs and share the rule with the class.

1. Some researchers believe that fossil fuels **can be** completely **replaced** by infinite sources of energy.
2. In some parts of our rain forests, there are no longer any trees. They **must have been cut down** and **used** as fuel or construction wood.
3. Some young Masai shepherds are unemployed because they are illiterate. They **should have been sent** to school when they were children.

4. Because that young man does not know how to approach a group of monkeys, researchers believe that he **could not have been cared for** by monkeys when he was a child.

5. World health and employment problems **cannot be explained** only in terms of education. Economic systems **must** also **be considered.**

Practice

D. Complete the sentences with the correct form and tense of the modal and main verbs in brackets.

1. A child aged eighteen months has more curiosity than a research scientist. For this reason, all small children _____ (should / encourage) by their parents to explore the world around them.

2. After reviewing the results of the IVF treatment, the scientists realized that the eggs _____ (must / implant) in the wrong woman.

3. Local people say that this child was brought up by wolves. Before any conclusions are reached, however, the child _____ (have to / test) by a team of feral child researchers.

4. Thanks to the use of polymers, the progression of many serious diseases _____ (might / block) in the next few years.

5. Because they do so much damage to the environment, Joseph Cargnelli believes that fossil fuels, _____ (should / replace) by alternative sources of energy years ago.

6. Those children were very foolish to cross that busy road. (they could/kill)

Passive of modal verbs

Example	Form	Meaning
That movie is in black and white. It *must have been made* a long time ago.	perfect aspect: modal verb + *have* + *been* + *past* participle	to express a strong supposition
Some analog chip design problems *can be solved* mathematically.	present tense: modal verb + *be* + past participle	to talk about something that is currently possible
The teacher is sick, so the class *will have to be postponed* until tomorrow.	future + *will* (applies only to *have to*): *will* + modal + *be* + past participle	to talk about a future necessity

Test yourself

E. For each of the statements, write a second sentence using a modal in either active or passive that explains or extends the first statement. Use the cues in brackets.

1. Look! Everybody is getting out umbrellas. (rain) _____

2. Those animals are now extinct. (protect) _____

3. John got home very late last night. (work late / visit his sister) _____

4. I'm not sure why Angela is late. (delay / bad weather) _____

5. E-mail communication is extremely fast. (send / in a question of seconds) _____

6. Many Masai shepherd children are very intelligent. (teach to read and write quickly) _____

7. Those buildings are extremely old. (build) _____

Using convincing reasons in oral presentations

When you are giving a presentation, you may sometimes need to convince your audience that the ideas you are presenting are justified, so make sure you give clear reasons. You can use phrases such as these.

This will work because …
The main benefits are …
This would improve …
in ways such as …

A. PAIR WORK What problems could technology solve in the future? What kinds of new inventions would help a lot of people in the world?

An opinion survey about world problems posed to Europeans under age thirty-five found that in Italy, people were most concerned about the environment, while people in the U.K. worried most about health and education. In France, under-thirty-five-year-olds said that unemployment and immigration were the most important problems.

B. Choose one of your ideas from exercise A and prepare a one- to two-minute presentation about an invention that we need now. In your presentation, keep these points in mind.

- describe the problem
- state what kind of technology or invention is needed
- explain the reasons why we need it
- explain how this technology would make people's lives better

To plan your presentation, first think about what you are going to say. Then make notes on paper. Remember, notes contain only the most important words and ideas.

C. PAIR WORK Practice with your partner. Take turns giving your presentations, listening, and giving feedback. Don't read your presentation aloud from the paper. Use your notes only if you forget what to say.

D. Give your presentation in front of the class. Remember to look at your audience and speak a little louder than normal.

E. CLASS TASK Discuss which of these new inventions you think we'll see in the next twenty years.

A. PAIR WORK Complete the text with one of the words or phrases from the box. Then form a group with another pair of students and compare your answers.

| stressful | benefits | for | nerve-wracking | hours |
| tedious | resigning | earns | paid | career |

Pete Cooper works **(1)** _____ an investment bank in New York. He **(2)** _____ an excellent salary but he has to work incredibly long **(3)** _____. Although his job comes with a lot of **(4)** _____, such as medical insurance and fifteen days' **(5)** _____ vacation, Pete is thinking of **(6)** _____ and setting up his own business. He feels that there are not enough **(7)** _____ prospects in his current position. He does the same old thing day in day out, and it has become rather **(8)** _____. Although working for himself might prove less **(9)** _____ than working for other people, Pete is aware that it could also be quite **(10)** _____, as he will not have the job security he has in his present position.

B. Read these sentences. Then complete statements 1 to 4 with one of the words in **bold.** You will have to use one of these words two times.

- I love my **job.** It's the **work** I hate!
- Charles is not interested in having an exciting **career.** All he wants is a steady **job.**
- Rosemary is planning a **career** in international development after college. She knows that she will find the **work** quite challenging, but this is what she wants.
- He's looking for **work** at the moment but unfortunately he is overqualified for all the **jobs** available.

1. _____ is used to refer to the position you have and for which you get paid.

2. _____ is used to refer to what you actually do on a daily basis when you are employed.

3. _____ is used to talk about a long period of time spent making progress in one profession.

4. _____ is used in the sense of *employment* or as a noncount form of *job.*

C. Complete these statements with *job, work,* or *career.*

1. Maggie began as a classroom teacher. Now she is a school director. She has had a very successful _____.

2. I hate this _____. The salary is low, the work is boring, and there are no benefits.

3. That doctor has completely ruined his _____ by selling medications to his patients.

4. Pamela resigned. She had so much _____ that she never had time for her family.

5. I'd love to have one of those _____ where you didn't have to do any work!

6. The boss says she's delighted with my _____ so I'm going to get a promotion.

D. GROUP WORK Take turns reading these work-related proverbs aloud and say what you think each one means. Then with the class, discuss whether there are similar proverbs in your language.

1. Many hands make light work.
2. Never put off till tomorrow what you can do today.
3. The Devil finds work for idle hands to do.
4. Too many cooks spoil the broth.
5. A handful of skill is better than a bagful of gold.
6. Rome wasn't built in a day.
7. The early bird catches the worm.
8. All work and no play makes Jack a dull boy.

Listening
strategy

Listening for examples

When a speaker uses a new or unusual term and you do not understand exactly what it means, pay careful attention to any examples provided. By listening to specific examples, you should get a clearer idea of what the term means.

Before you listen

A. PAIR WORK What electrical appliances do you use every day? Do any of them have computers inside? Why are some cars fitted with computers?

First listening

B. Listen to interviews with three people about a new kind of technology called "pervasive computing." Match each speaker's name with an opinion.

1. Russell Chao _____

2. Leah Feldman _____

3. William Groves _____

   a. Companies should study which pervasive computing products people really want.

   b. Pervasive computing is already solving many important world problems.

   c. Engineers should not waste their time working on pervasive computing.

   d. Consumers will only buy pervasive computing products if they're practical.

   e. Pervasive computing will be able to do more important things in the future.

Second listening

C. Listen again and take notes on examples of pervasive computing appliances and what they can do.

After listening

D. Do you agree with any of these speakers? Do any of the products they described sound interesting or useful to you? Is pervasive computing a good idea?

Test yourself

E. Listen to the final section of the program about pervasive computing and answer the question.

What is the speaker's opinion about videophones?

   a. They are a good example of pervasive computing.

   b. They will be increasingly common in the future.

   c. They are an example of unsuccessful technology.

   d. They prove how important computers are today.

Writing an academic essay

Before you write

A. GROUP WORK First make a list of the six most serious problems you think the world could face in the next twenty years if no action is taken. Identify and list ten occupations or professions that might help us cope with these problems. Give your reasons for each choice. Then imagine twenty years have passed. Some of the problems have been solved and others have not. Complete the chart.

Problems solved   **Reason problem was solved**
Unsolved problems   **Reason problem was not solved**

Write

B. In the same groups, use the chart to write a four-paragraph essay in which you argue a case for one of the following positions.

a. In twenty years' time, our world will be a much better place to live in.

b. In twenty years' time, our world will be a much worse place to live in.

Plan the essay very well. Remember, it must consist of these parts.

- **Introductory paragraph.** Use a preamble sentence(s) and a sentence showing the position you are going to take.
- **Supporting paragraphs.** These should contain very specific information to support the position you adopt in the introductory paragraph.
- **Concluding paragraph.** This needs to summarize the main ideas of the essay.

C. Join another group and exchange essays. Discuss the content and make suggestions for improvement. Then in the same groups you worked in on exercise B, put the finishing touches to your essay and elect a member of your group to read the essay to the whole class. Comment on the content of the essays of the other groups.

A. GROUP WORK Read the situations and for each situation, comment on, criticize, or speculate about the behavior described.

EXAMPLE:

> *1. Last night our elderly neighbors started to play loud dance music at 2 a.m.*
> *They must not have realized what time it was.*
> *They might have a teenage visitor in their house.*
> *They may have switched the CD player on by mistake.*

1. Last night, our elderly neighbors started to play loud dance music at 2 a.m.
2. My friend in Korea hasn't sent me an e-mail in weeks.
3. I sent my best friend a birthday present and still haven't received a thank-you note.
4. I saw one of the students from our class get in a taxi the other day with a lot of baggage.
5. Our English teacher looked very unhappy this morning.
6. My Japanese friends are coming to see me in the States next summer.
7. The president of our country is returning early from a vacation.
8. One of my closest friends called and asked me for help last night, but I was so busy I didn't have a lot of time to talk.

B. Do you know of any unsolved mysteries in the history of your country, community, or family? If you do, get into a group of four with three people who do not have an unsolved mystery to tell. Tell your story to the other three students and listen to the speculations they make about the mystery. Then select a member of your group to tell the unsolved mystery to the class and to share all the speculations you made. With the whole class, discuss the mysteries and identify the one that is most difficult to explain.

C. CLASS TASK Skim the readings in Units 1–12 of *In Detail 2*. Then work with a partner and choose texts for each of these categories.

- the most philanthropic person you learned about
- the most worrying piece of information
- the most incredible story
- the most exciting scientific breakthrough
- the most interesting animal
- the most informative text
- the most admirable person or people
- the most fascinating fact

For more detail about Achievement, view the CNN video. Activities to accompany the video begin on page 145.

Join another pair of students and try to reach an agreement about the points above. Then share your conclusions with the whole class and have a short debate about each one to see if the whole class can reach a general agreement.

Review Your Grammar

A. Circle the word in parentheses that correctly completes each sentence.

1. I don't know (that, who, whom) the man in the black shirt is.
2. I am sure (that, who, whom) it is after 10:00.
3. Can you tell me (that, who, whom) she is?
4. Arnold Meyer, (that, which, whom) I have never met, wrote me a letter.
5. Tell me something (that, who, whom) I don't already know.
6. My cousin, (that, which, whose) boyfriend I really like, hasn't called me in weeks.

B. Complete each sentence with the correct verb form from the box.

have been   will be (2)   will have to be   will have been   will have

1. Soon everyone _____ carrying a hand-held computer.
2. By next August, I _____ living here for six years.
3. If you want to go with me, you _____ on time.
4. I'm not sure, but I think that chair must _____ made a long time ago.
5. By 11:00, everyone _____ putting their coats on and leaving.
6. When I come back from vacation next month, I _____ used up all my vacation days for this year.

High Challenge

C. Write the letter of the correct word or phrase in the blank.

1. By the year 2080, people _____ cell phones for 100 years.
   a. will be using   **b.** will have been using   **c.** will use   **d.** will be used

2. Within twenty years, most people_____ smoking.
   a. will have stopped   **b.** will have been stopped   **c.** would have stopped
   d. will be stopped

3. People _____ jobs are dangerous often live with high stress levels.
   a. that   **b.** who   **c.** whose   **d.** which

4. Last week I saw a great movie, the name _____ I've forgotten.
   a. whose   **b.** that   **c.** which   **d.** of which

5. The car accident _____ by the rainy weather.
   a. must cause   **b.** must be caused   **c.** must have caused   **d.** must have been caused

6. I can't find my ID card, so I _____ a new one.
   a. had to get   **b.** will have to get   **c.** must have gotten   **d.** must be gotten

Review Your Vocabulary

A. Circle the word that doesn't belong.

1. abuse disregard encourage hurt
2. punish smile wink nod
3. sibling brother volunteer sister
4. adventurous repressive innovative creative
5. enthusiasm boredom excitement interest
6. shepherd educator genius expert

B. Match each sentence with its communication goals a to e.

___ 1. By a year from now, prices will probably have risen.

___ 2. I went to three stores before I could find a spreadsheet program that I liked.

___ 3. Finding inexpensive computer software requires careful research.

___ 4. Remember to follow these three steps before you buy: talk to friends, look at several catalogs, and try shopping online.

___ 5. Spreadsheet programs cost from $100 to $800.

a. introduce a topic
b. give a supporting detail
c. give a short summary
d. predict a future event
e. narrate an experience

C. Check ([insert check mark]) the best response.

1. Are you working very hard at your new job?
   ___ Yes, it's a part-time job.
   ___ Yes, they really put me through my paces.
2. What are your employers doing?
   ___ They're launching a company.
   ___ They're entering a company.
3. What should you do when you see an opportunity?
   ___ Optimize it.
   ___ Punish it.
4. What happens when the company loses a lot of money?
   ___ It's very motivating.
   ___ It's very debilitating.
5. Is the company looking for people to invest money?
   ___ Yes, they're making a public offering.
   ___ Yes, they're giving the employees more benefits.
6. Why was Sylvia fired?
   ___ She was very efficient.
   ___ She was too temperamental.

FYI

At an advanced level of English, you need the right resources at hand to help you as you study. Having a good bilingual dictionary, a good learner's dictionary, and a good grammar reference book is very important.

Review Your Speaking

Fluency

A. PAIR WORK Take turns describing one of the pictures and then discuss whether it is necessary to have a formal ceremony to mark an important occasion.

B. GROUP WORK Prepare a presentation about a current situation in your life and how it will change in the next few years. You might discuss educational issues, your status at work, or a personal situation. Make notes on the chart. Then tell your group about the situation and answer any questions they may have.

Topic	
Main idea 1	
Example, explanations, details relating to main idea 1	
Main idea 2	
Example, explanations, details relating to main idea 2	
Conclusion	

F•A•Q

Can watching TV and videos in English really help me improve my speaking?

This can be a useful activity. You will become more used to the sound of English and may also pick up some new words and phrases. Although learning English is generally hard work, watching TV or movies may be a relaxing and fun way for you to absorb more language.

Review Your Listening

A. GROUP WORK Discuss these questions in a group. Do you think you received a good education in your earlier years? Why or why not? What "grade" would you give your elementary school? What "grade" would you give your high school?

Listening 1

B. You are going to hear a debate about how to improve education. Listen to the first part and write down each person's main idea in your own words. Remember to ask yourself if you will need to listen for general or specific information.

C. Listen again, and first, take notes on each speaker's recommendations for better schools. You will complete the chart in exercise D.

Speaker	Recommendations	Other speaker's response to these recommendations
Dr. Gibbs		
Mr. Clark		

Listening 2

D. Now you will hear the two speakers reacting to each other. Take notes on their responses to the other speaker's recommendations.

E. Listen again and try to work out the meaning of the word *curriculum*.

F. Do you agree with either of these speakers? How do you think schools in your country could be improved?

Video Worksheets

Unit 1: Christopher Reeve

Before viewing

A. PAIR WORK Imagine you were suddenly unable to walk and had to use a wheelchair to get around. Which parts of your present daily life would be the same? Which would be more difficult? Which would be impossible?

B. You are going to watch a video interview with Christopher Reeve. Check the meaning of the expressions in the box.

> It's up my alley.   IC unit
> I see light at the end of the tunnel.
> wishful thinking

First viewing

C. Watch the video and check Reeve's activities.

directing a movie____

writing a book ____

working with children ____

traveling ____

visiting patients in hospitals ____

raising money ____

Second viewing

D. Watch again and find this information.

1. the new kind of work that Reeve did recently ____
2. the name of the charity he works with ____
3. the place where this charity held their event ____
4. the name of another actor who is working with Reeve ____
5. the number of Americans who have the same problem as Reeve ____

After viewing

E. Talk about these questions.

1. Which of Reeve's activities in the video surprises you the most? Why?
2. In your opinion, why has Reeve been able to do so many things?
3. How difficult is life for people who use wheelchairs in your country? What could be done to make it easier?

Unit 2: A Home away from Home

Before viewing

A. PAIR WORK What kinds of people have to travel a lot for their work? How do you think they feel about this? Imagine that you were offered a job that would require you to be away from home three weeks out of every month. Would you accept it? Why or why not?

B. You are going to watch a video about inexpensive hotels for business travelers in the U.S. Check the meaning of the words in the box.

> downtown   suburban
> amenity

First viewing

C. Watch the video and check the features that are offered at these hotels.

microwave ovens in the rooms ____

luxury restaurants ____

top-quality service ____

voice mail ____

free breakfast ____

workspace in the rooms ____

free guided tours ____

Second viewing

D. Watch again and find this information.

1. another term for a suburban business hotel ____
2. a guest's opinion of a room at a suburban business hotel ____
3. the usual price of a room in a downtown business hotel ____
4. the usual price of a room in a suburban business hotel ____

After viewing

E. Talk about these questions.

1. Why are these hotels cheaper than downtown hotels? What kinds of travelers would prefer each kind of hotel?
2. Would hotels like the ones in the video be popular in your country? Why or why not?
3. When you travel, where do you like to stay? Why?

Unit 3: Ant Farms

Before viewing

A. PAIR WORK What do you know about ants? Share information about their size, food and habitat.

B. You are going to watch a video about plastic "homes" for ants, called ant farms. Why might a person want to keep ants?

C. Check the meaning of the words in the box.

enthusiast (n)　tunnel
captivity

First viewing

D. Read the statements, then watch the video and circle True (T) or False (F).

1. Ant farms are a new idea. T　F
2. Ant farms are mainly a toy for children. T　F
3. Uncle Milton Industries is a big business. T　F
4. One man collects all the ants for the ant farms. T　F
5. You can keep the same ants for a long time. T　F
6. Uncle Milton Industries makes other products. T　F

Second viewing

E. Watch again and fill in the spaces.

"But the ____Milton Levine formed with his brother-in-law in the 40s was no ____at all. Together they came up with the ____. Before long Levine was ____as Uncle Milton and his Ant Farm was a smash."

  "And this is the operation. Ken Fawcett, ant ____, armed with a straw to blow the ants out of their ____, legged with socks on the outside to protect himself from the stings of renegades, his bounty about a penny an ant, or about ____dollars a year when you add up the ____ants he collects and sends off to ant farm ____."

After viewing

F. Talk about these questions.

1. What can a person learn by observing ants closely?
2. Did you have any pets as a child? If so, what did you learn from your pet?
3. Would you like to have an ant farm at home? Why or why not?

Unit 4: Urban Migration

Before viewing

A. PAIR WORK What do you know about China, its people, and its economy? Look at your clothes, shoes, and the possessions you have with you. Are any of them made in China?

B. You are going to watch a video about Chinese people who have moved from the countryside to Beijing. Check the meaning of the words in the box.

| textile | sector | hurdle |

First viewing

C. Read these questions, then watch the video and choose the correct answers.

1. What is the migrants' situation in Beijing?
   a. It is not legal for them to live there.
   b. The government has invited them there.
   c. They have relatives who live there.
   d. They are permitted to stay for a short time.

2. Why are the migrants important for Beijing?
   a. They spend a lot of money.
   b. They work hard for low pay.
   c. They are well educated.
   d. They diversify the culture.

3. How do the natives of Beijing feel about the migrants?
   a. They welcome the migrants.
   b. They think the migrants take away their jobs.
   c. They often try to help the migrants.
   d. They think the migrants cause social problems.

4. What has the government done about education for the migrants' children?
   a. It has built inexpensive new schools.
   b. It has sent the children back to their hometowns.
   c. It has destroyed schools built by the migrants.
   d. It has sent migrants to the university.

Second viewing

D. Watch again and fill in the spaces.

The ____ is not completely bleak. This nongovernment organization is part of a small but growing ____ to teach migrants urban survival skills and to give them the feeling that they have contributed to Beijing's ____. Legal advice is aimed at women migrants who ____ the most systematic exploitation by employers.

Meanwhile the uncounted and the ____ are still lured to the city, where there are opportunities to make money but not to make a ____.

After viewing

E. Talk about these questions.

1. What things are probably difficult for these people to adjust to?

2. In your country, do people move from the countryside to major cities? What are the advantages of living in each place?

3. Do you think governments should try to control where their citizens live? Why or why not?

Unit 5: Noncitizens in the United States

Before viewing

A. PAIR WORK Are there foreigners living in your country? Why do they come to your country? Do you think life is easier or more difficult for them than it is in their native countries?

B. You are going to watch a video about Shen Kim, a Korean man living in the U.S. Check the meaning of the words in the box.

crack down
enforcement   deported

First viewing

C. Watch the video and take notes about these things.

Shen Kim's business ____
what the law says ____
how Shen Kim feels ____

Second viewing

D. Watch again and circle True (T) or False (F).

1. Shen Kim is an American citizen. T   F

2. He thinks the law is unjust. T   F

3. This law was made recently. T   F

4. Noncitizens must report their address to the government. T   F

5. Noncitizens can be sent home if they don't obey this law. T   F

6. Attorneys think this is a good way to catch terrorists. T   F

7. The U.S. government has not enforced such rules in the past. T   F

8. There is a well-organized system to keep track of foreigners. T   F

After viewing

E. Talk about these questions.

1. Do you agree with Shen Kim's opinion? Why or why not?

2. What rights should people have when they are living in another country?

Unit 6: Pollution Control: Athens Metro

Before viewing

A. PAIR WORK Do you ever use public transportation? Why or why not? What are some advantages of buses, trains, and subways? Have you even ridden on a subway?

B. You are going to watch a video about a new subway line in Athens. Check the meaning of the words in the box.

collapsed   finds (n) archeological assert

First viewing

C. Watch the video and take notes on these things.

problems building the new subway line _____
what they found during construction _____
why the new line was built _____

Second viewing

D. Watch again and find these numbers in the video.

1. the cost of the project in dollars ____

2. the depth of the tunnels, in stories ____

3. the population of Greece ____

4. the year when subway construction began ____

5. the number of original stations ____

6. the number of stations added in the new metro ____

7. the year of the Athens Olympic Games ____

After viewing

E. Talk about these questions.

1. What surprised you the most in the video?

2. If your city built a new subway station or train station, how would you like to decorate it?

3. What would be the best way to improve public transportation in your city?

Unit 7: Canine Translator

Before viewing

A. PAIR WORK How do animals communicate with people? Do you have a pet? Do you think it communicates with you?

B. You are going to watch a video about a new invention to help people understand dogs. Check the meaning of the words in the box.

wag   growl   bark   whine

First viewing

C. Read these statements, then watch the video and circle True (T) or False (F).

1. The Bow-lingual was invented in Japan. T   F
2. It interprets dogs' words and phrases. T   F
3. The dog wears a microphone. T   F
4. The invention tells you about your dog's feelings. T   F
5. At the end of the day, it gives you a list. T   F
6. This invention can translate into many languages. T   F

Second viewing

D. Watch again and fill in the spaces.

When he whines or barks, it senses the timbre of the bark and translates that into the dog's ____. The information is then sent to what is ____the Canine Emotion Pager. The Pager tells you what the barks ____in terms of human emotions, like anger, frustration, even a ____of accomplishment. After collecting data from a full ____of barking, Bow-lingual will give the owners a list of their dog's emotions using ____ preprogrammed sentences. Bow-lingual is expected to go on sale this coming ____ for just over a hundred dollars.

After viewing

E. Talk about these questions.

1. Do you think the inventors were serious? Why or why not?
2. Is this invention useful?
3. If dogs could really talk, what kinds of things might they talk about? What about cats? Horses?

Unit 8: United Airlines Troubles

Before viewing

A. PAIR WORK Have you ever traveled by plane? Did you have any problems? What kinds of problems do people sometimes have on plane trips?

B. You are going to watch a video about problems caused by a pilots' strike at an airline. Check the meaning of these words: marooned labor contract flash point frustration

First viewing

C. Watch the video and find this information.

1. Which airline had the strike?
2. How do the airline's customers feel?
3. What did the airline's CEO do?
4. How is the airline trying to get its customers back?
5. Are customers more satisfied with other airlines?

Second viewing

D. What happened first? Number this sequence of events in logical order. Then watch the video again to check.

____ More people go to the airport.

____ People feel frustrated.

____ The economy is booming.

____ Web sites sell more cheap plane tickets.

____ Airport lines are longer.

____ More people want to travel.

After viewing

E. Talk about these questions.

1. What should a company do when its customers are dissatisfied?
2. Would you like to work in the airline industry? Why or why not?
3. Imagine you are the CEO of an airline. How would you make your airline different from and better than all the others? Think about planes, routes, service, etc.

Unit 9: Conjoined Twin Judgment

Before viewing

| devout   abdomen |
| spine   lungs |

A. You are going to watch a video about a pair of conjoined twins. Twins like these are born with their bodies joined together. Check the meaning of the words in the box.

B. PAIR WORK What kinds of problems would conjoined twins have? What are some reasons for separating them? Some reasons for leaving them joined together? Have there been any cases like this in your country?

First viewing

C. Watch the video and find this information.

1. Do doctors want the twins separated?
2. Do their parents want the twins separated?
3. What will happen if they are separated?
4. What will happen if they are not separated?
5. Who will decide?

Second viewing

D. Watch again and fill in the spaces.

DOCTOR: It's a fundamental ____ ____ issue. After this, foreign nationals coming to this country seeking ____ advice, they should be able to go wherever they want for another medical ____ rather than this team's grabbing them and putting a court order saying "We will ____."

REPORTER: There are no easy ____ for the judges who say their decision is all the more complicated with no ____ precedent here or in other common law countries to ____ them.

After viewing

E. Talk about these questions.

1. In your opinion, what should be done with these babies?
2. Who should have the right to make medical decisions about small children: their parents, their doctors, judges?

Unit 10: Personal Heroes

Before viewing

A. PAIR WORK Do you have any personal heroes? If so, who are they? Why do you admire them?

B. You are going to watch a video in which several people talk about their personal heroes. Which of the names in the box have you heard of?

James Lovell
Sammy Sosa
Jackie Robinson
Ed Begley
Charles Lindbergh
Roberto Clemente
César Chávez

First viewing

C. Watch the video and take notes on these things.

Jim Lovell's ideas about why heroes are important _____

Sammy Sosa's heroes _____

how Sammy Sosa's heroes inspired him _____

Second viewing

D. Watch again and fill in the spaces.

When I hear the word ____ I think of César Chávez. He was an incredible man because of the way he ____. He was not looking out for ____ ____, and putting money away somewhere. He lived the way ____ ____ lived. And he fought for social justice, for environmental justice. And he is one of the great ____ . . . He's the greatest hero I've ever ____ in my life.

After viewing

E. Talk about these questions.

1. In your opinion, who is the greatest hero of your country? Why?
2. Did you have any heroes when you were a child? Do you still admire these people?
3. Why do you think people have heroes?

Unit 11: Masai Gift

Before viewing

A. PAIR WORK Do you know anyone who has studied in another country? Would you like to do this? What can people learn from studying overseas?

B. You are going to watch a video about a student from Kenya who wanted to help Americans. Check the meaning of the words in the box.

cattle   tragedy
solidarity   sympathy
commission (v)

First viewing

C. Watch the video and answer these questions.

1. Where was the student on September 11, 2001?
2. Why was he in the U.S.?
3. What did he do after he went back to his hometown?
4. What did the people in his hometown decide to do?

Second viewing

D. Watch again and match the sentence parts.

1. The student wanted to help   **a.**
                                        b.
2. The Masai people gave the cattle   **c.**
                                        d.
3. The ambassador went to the village   **e.**
4. The cattle were sold

5. The money from the cattle was used

After viewing

E. Talk about these questions.

1. What is your reaction to this gift? Do you think it was a good idea?
2. How can international students help other countries?

Unit 12: Young Inventors

Before viewing

A. PAIR WORK Which household chores are the hardest? How did people do these things 100 years ago? Which modern inventions save the most work at home?

pedal (*n* and *v*)
prototype   portable
durable

B. You are going to watch a video about a new invention developed by students. Check the meaning of the words in the box.

First viewing

C. Watch the video and answer these questions.

1. What does the machine do?
2. How does it work?
3. Who was the machine designed for?
4. How much would it cost?

Second viewing

D. Watch again and take notes on these things.

advantages of the machine _____

what the inventors must do next _____

After viewing

C. Talk about these questions.

1. Do you think this invention would be useful? Why or why not? Would people in your country use it?
2. What kinds of inventions could help people in developing countries?
3. What new invention would improve your life the most?

Perfect progressives

Use the perfect progressive (present, past, or future) in the following two cases:

1. To describe a continuous or repetitive activity that occurs before another point in time (the continuous activity is in the progressive):

Past perfect progressive

*I **had been thinking** about you when you called.*

Present perfect progressive

*I **have been considering** your job offer.*

Future perfect progressive

*By the time you get home to Singapore, we **will have been working** in Boston for four hours.*

2. To describe a continuous activity with temporary effects:

Past perfect progressive

*I could tell she **had been crying** because her eyes were red.*

Present perfect progressive

*He **has been eating** onions and I can smell them on his breath!*

Wish *clauses*

We use hypothetical statements with *wish* to talk about situations that are not true or not likely to become true.

Statement	Implied meaning
*I **wish** you **had come** to the lake last weekend.*	*You didn't come.*
*I **wish** you **liked** Thai food.*	*You don't like it.*
*I **wish** you **could come** to my party.*	*You refuse to come.*

Only *for emphasis*

Placing the word only *at the beginning of a sentence does not change the essential meaning. It simply adds emphasis to the phrase that comes immediately after it.*

***Only** after living abroad do most students realize how much they love their own countries.*

When *only* is placed at the beginning of a sentence, the subject and verb in the main clause are always inverted.

Subject and object complements

Complements	Notes
Subject complements	
1. Joyce seems *happy.* (adjective)	A subject complement describes the subject. An intransitive verb links the subject and its complement.
2. Joyce is *an aerobics instructor.* (noun phrase)	A subject complement can be (1) an adjective, (2) a noun phrase, (3) an infinitive phrase, or (4) a noun clause.
3. Her dream is *to have two fitness centers.* (infinitive phrase)	
4. Fitness is *what she really believes in.* (noun clause)	

Complements | Notes

Object complements

Complements	Notes
1. Many people consider *aerobics the best workout*. 　　　　　　(dir. obj.)　　(obj. comp.)	An object complement describes the direct object. Verbs such as *consider, find, call, imagine,* and *prove,* which reflect the
2. Mary finds *aerobics exhausting*. 　　　　(dir. obj.) (obj. comp.)	opinion or perception of the speaker, take noun or adjective object complements as in (1) and (2).
3. Some magazines labeled *the 80s the decade of fitness*. 　　　　　　　　(dir. obj.)　　(obj. comp.)	Verbs such as *call, label,* and *name,* which indicate a name or label for the object, take noun object complements as in (3).
4. Many people regard *the fitness craze* as a *wake-up call*. 　　　　　　(dir. obj.)　　　(obj. comp.)	A few verbs that are followed by *as* or *for* are followed by object complements as in (4), e.g., *recognize, regard, accept, mistake, take, describe.*

Infinitives of purpose in initial position

Example	Notes
To travel to Mars would take months.	The infinitive subject is more formal.
It would take months **to travel** *to Mars.*	Using *it* as the subject is much more common than using an infinitive.

Relative adverbs

Relative adverbs *where, when, why,* and *how* can replace prepositions + the relative pronoun *which* when these prepositions refer to place, time, reason, or manner.

Relative adverb	Meaning	Replaces preposition + *which*
A spa is a place **where** *you go either to exercise or relax.* (to which)	place	*to* *at*
Summer is the time **when** *many people take vacations.* (during which)	time	*from which* *in*
A reason **why** *some people move to large cities from small towns is to find jobs.* (for which)	reason	*during* *at* *in which*
I like **how** *you wrote your paper.* (the way in which)	manner	*on* *for which* *(the way) in which*

Note: When *how* replaces *in which,* you must also delete the noun phrase *the way* before it.

Relative adverb clauses often modify nouns. The noun is called a head noun because it is the head of the clause that follows.

The head noun is often a general word such as *place, time,* or *reason,* but it can also be a more specific word, especially for places and times.

Head Noun	+	Relative adverb	+	Clause
a place		where		you can relax
a time		when		I can call you
a reason		why		you should go

Stative and dynamic passives

Dynamic passives	Stative passives	Notes
The missing library book **was found** in the parking lot by a custodian.	A map of Los Angeles **can be found** on the Internet.	Many verbs can be either stative or dynamic depending on their meaning. Dynamic passive verbs describe activities. Stative passive verbs do not report activities; they express states or conditions. Stative passive verbs do not have agents.
Our telephone line **is being connected** by tomorrow.	The transmission of a car **is connected** to the gearshift.	
Jean **was called** for a job interview yesterday.	Temperature **is measured** in degrees.	

Complex passives

Complex passives are passive constructions followed by *that* clauses or infinitive clauses (*to* + verb).

Examples	Notes
It **is believed** that primates first appeared on the earth about sixty-nine million years ago.	**Form:** Introductory *it* + passive verb + *that* clause **Use:** This form often serves to introduce a topic, since the new information comes at the end of the sentence.
The topic for today is early primates. Primates **are believed** to have appeared on the earth about sixty-nine million years ago.	**Form:** Subject (other than introductory *it*) + passive verb + *to* infinitive **Use:** This form could also be used to introduce topics, but it is especially appropriate after a topic has been introduced because the topic can be put in the subject position.

Reduced adverb clause

Adverb clauses of **time, reason,** and **opposition** can be reduced to adverb phrases without any change in meaning.

Clauses of time

> **Clause: While she was at college,** *she exercised every day.*
> **Phrase: (While) being at college,** *she exercised every day.*

Notes

The subjects of both clauses must be the same; otherwise, reduction isn't possible.

The verb form is changed to a participle *-ing* in the reduced phrase.

Keeping the subordinator *(while)* is optional in the reduction.

Clauses of reason

> **Clause: Because she was a good student,** *she received a scholarship.*
> **Phrase: Being a good student,** *she received a scholarship.*

Notes

The subject and the subordinator are deleted.

The verb is changed to verb *+-ing.*

Clauses of opposition

> **Clause:** *Although she was happy at college,* **she missed her family.**
> **Phrase:** *Although happy at college,* **she missed her family.**

Notes:

The subject and *be* are deleted.

The subordinator and the adjective are kept.

Causative verbs

Examples

let, make, help, have

These verbs express cause and are followed by a noun or pronoun and the infinitive form of the verb, adjective, or participle.

Verbs and structures	Examples	Meanings
make + (pro)noun + infinitive (omit *to*) + (pro)noun + adjective	My teacher **makes me write** an essay every week. Taking tests **makes me nervous.**	require, force cause a physical or emotional reaction
have + (pro)noun + infinitive form	Kathy **has her kids clean** their rooms on Saturdays.	delegate work or responsibility
let + (pro)noun + infinitive form	Never **let a stranger carry** your bags at the airport.	allow, enable
get + (pro)noun + to + infinitve	We should **get our teacher to go out** with us Friday night.	persuade
help + (pro)noun + infinitive form + (pro)noun + infinitive form	Writing **helps me express** myself.	provide assistance in making something happen

In a passive construction, the causative verb is followed by a noun or pronoun and a participle.

*Kathy **has her house cleaned** every Saturday.*

Definite, indefinite, and zero article— making generalizations

Count nouns		
Form	**Use**	**Examples**
the + singular noun	Use *the* when speaking generally about nouns in the following categories: plants, animals, technical inventions, and with certain adjectives used as nouns (e.g., *the rich*).	*The computer has changed everyday life in the United States.* *The rich get richer and the poor get poorer.*
the + plural noun	Use *the* when speaking generally about nouns in the following categories: classes of people (ethnic groups, professional groups) and plural proper nouns.	*The Native Americans lost their land.* *The doctors have special privileges.*
a/an + singular noun	For nouns that do not belong in any of the categories described above, use *a/an* when making generalizations about those nouns.	*A car is a necessity in the city.*
plural noun with no article (0)	Nouns can also be made plural and used without an article to make generalizations in less formal usage. Note: It is not possible to use *the* with these plural nouns for generalizations.	*Cars are necessary in this city.* **Incorrect:** *The cars are necessary in this city.*

Non-count nouns

zero article	**Never** use an article with a non-count noun when making a generalization.	**Examples** *Love is a many-splendored thing.* *Gold is a precious metal.* *Death and taxes are inevitable.*

Future forms

Forms	Examples	Uses
Simple present	*Kay **completes** her studies next May.*	definite future plans or schedules
Present progressive	*I **am leaving** at 7:00 A.M. tomorrow.*	future intentions
Be going to future	*The movie **is going to start** in a few minutes.*	probable and immediate future events
Simple future	*I **will help** you with your homework tonight.*	willingness, promises
Future progressive	*John's family **will be coming** to visit him this summer.*	events that will be in progress in the near future
Future perfect	*His family **will have left** home before the rainy season.*	before a certain time in the future
Future perfect progressive	*By the end of this year, I **will have been studying** English for three years.*	up until a certain time in the future

Glossary

Word	Definition
abuse	unfair or bad treatment
abusive	insulting
accounted for	explained with reference to
acquisition target	investment
adopt	take legal responsibility for a child who is not your own
are looking into	are examining
are pushing ahead with	are pursuing
authority	person in control
awarded	given a prize
benefits	valuable service or privilege provided to an employee by an employer in addition to salary
betraying	not being true to, being disloyal to
blackout	failure of electricity
bright spark	very intelligent person
bursting of a bubble	dramatic end to a period of rapid economic growth
career	a life's work, especially in business or in a profession
careless	inattentive to detail
cassava	African root vegetable
catch on	sell well
caught up	have all one's work done
childless	not having had a child
close down	go out of business
collapse	sudden failure of
college entrance exams	tests to gain entry to a college or university
concentrate	focus one's attention
cop	informal word for police officer
cripple	limit greatly
critics	people who complain about or find fault with something
crucial	extremely important
cut	not go to classes at a school or college
disrupts	causes disorder or malfunctioning
doubtless	without doubt, certainly
drives	motivates
earns	gets money by working
encouraged	gave strength or hope to someone
endowed	provided for permanent economic support
engage in	be involved, participate
enormous ego	high opinion of oneself
exploded	increased very dramatically
expresses	contains (scientific term)
failed	did not succeed
fees	charge, cost, payment
fleece	a woolly coat of certain animals like sheep and goats
flout	ignore with great pleasure
for	in the interest of
fruitless	without benefit, useless
genome	a particular number and combination of certain chromosomes, forming the single nucleus of a living cell
get a buzz out of	enjoy enormously

Word	Definition
get A grades	receive the highest grades at school
go it alone	survive without help
gobbling up	eating quickly and voraciously
going got tough	situation became challenging
goofed off	didn't work hard
got into trouble	did illegal acts, engaged in unlawful behavior
highly focused	center one's attention with great concentration
hopeless	without hope
hours	time period designated for certain activity
hygiene	science of personal health, especially cleanliness
hypersensitivity	higher degree of sensitivity
implication	suggestion, theoretical outcome
improve in	become better at something
in vain	without success
inadequate	incompetent
innovative	extremely creative
insist	say emphatically
inspiring	cause to work hard or be creative
insurance	protection against damage or loss
is carried out	studies
job	work that one is paid to do every day
kowtow	obey without questioning
latent	present but not yet developed
lead to	cause
livestock	farm animals
make an A	receive the highest grade
maltreatment	cruelty
monopoly	control of an entire market by one person or company
motivating	gives a reason to do something
mutations	genetic changes
nameless	without a name or with an unknown name
negligent	careless in doing one's duty
nerve-wracking	stressful, causing fear and tiredness
nod	move head up and down in agreement
optimize	use fully
orphan	child whose parents are dead
orphaned	not having parents
paid	gave money to someone in return for regular work
palm	the flat inner part of the hand
part time	taking up only part of a normal workday or workweek
participate	take part or have a role in an activity or event
patent	exclusive, legal right to an invention or process
pharmaceutical	related to medicines
philanthropic	unselfish, looking to help other people of society in general
pickled	preserved in liquid
pointless	meaningless, not worth doing
prejudice	unfair dislike of something or somebody

Word	Definition
pressure groups	groups of people who try to influence public opinion and government action
principal	head of a school
printing press	large machine for printing the written word
privileged	with cultural and economic advantages
prototype	produce the first model of something
puff	very small amount of wind
punished	made to pay for doing something wrong
put through...paces	try out, test
put up	offer
quest	search
relentless	never ending
repeat an exam	take the same test again
repressive	unreasonably strict
resigning	choosing to leave one's job or post
root	the part of the plant that grows into the ground and feeds the plant
set up	start
shady	protecting from sunlight
shoot up	increase quickly
simian	referring to or like a monkey
spare	do without
speak out against	protest about
status quo	the way things are now
stressful	causing worry or tension
strike	when workers refuse to work for a specific purpose
swollen	greatly increased
take on	employ
team up with	join
tedious	boring, long, and dull
temperamental	not very reliable, unpredictable
think the unthinkable	having new ideas
tighten up on	limit
tip of the iceberg	the small beginnings of something much larger
trust	organization with legal powers to take care of someone's property
tumor	a growth of diseased tissue
turn into	become
undisciplined	not showing control over mind or body
unruly	disobedient, loud, and wild
unwittingly	unintentionally
useless	worthless
volatility	unpredictability
walk out	stop working
wink	close and open an eye quickly
with flying colors	something that is done very well
wood	small forest
work	employment
work my way	move slowly
work out	understand
working on	trying to discover a solution